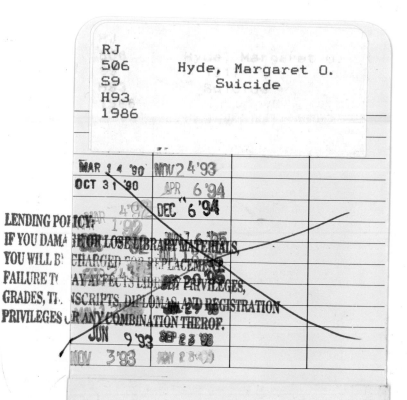

FEB 20 '90

SUICIDE

THE HIDDEN EPIDEMIC

SUICIDE

MARGARET O. HYDE
AND
ELIZABETH HELD
FORSYTH, M.D.

REVISED EDITION

Franklin Watts 1986
New York/London/Toronto/Sydney

Grateful acknowledgment is made for permission to
reprint from "Hopelessness: An Indicator of Suicidal Risk,"
by M. Kovacs, A. T. Beck, and M. A. Weissman, published
in *Suicide*, vol. 5, no. 2, copyright © 1975. The authors
would also like to thank the American Association of
Suicidology for providing the list of suicide-prevention centers.

Library of Congress Cataloging-in-Publication Data

Hyde, Margaret Oldroyd, 1917–
Suicide: the hidden epidemic.

Bibliography: p.
Includes index.
Summary: Discusses the problem of teenage suicide,
some theories about causes and patterns of suicidal
behavior, society's responses to suicide, and some
preventive measures.
1. Youth—Suicidal behavior—Juvenile literature.
2. Suicide—Prevention—Juvenile literature.   3. Crisis
intervention (Psychiatry)—United States—Directories.
[1. Suicide] I. Forsyth, Elizabeth Held. II. Title.
RJ506.S9H93   1986   616.85′8445   86-11039
              ISBN 0-531-10251-3

CONTENTS

SUICIDE

CHAPTER

1

TEEN SUICIDE: A GROWING EPIDEMIC

Right now, someone you know may be trying to die. Chances are good that person isn't even sure he wants to die. But he, or she, may succeed. You may never hear about a suicide attempt by someone you know. Most attempts are kept secret. However, if a friend tells you about ideas about suicide, or any suicide plans, you can be absolutely sure this is one secret that you must not keep. Ask for help from a crisis center or hotline, a doctor, teacher, clergyman, or anyone else trained to help suicidal people. A quick reaction may mean the difference between life and death. It may prevent your friend from becoming another statistic in a newly recognized, perhaps growing number of suicide deaths among the young. The idea is alarming.

When a teenager died in a car accident, it drew attention to seven other young people who took their own lives within the year. This was in the affluent suburb of Plano, near Dallas, Texas. In Westchester County, New York, where there were thirty teen suicides in a period of two years, five teenagers ended their lives within a twenty-day period. In Clear Lake, Texas, six teenagers committed suicide between February, 1983, and April, 1984. News reports about "cluster suicides" alarm communities far and wide. Some ask if suicide might, in some mysterious way, be contagious.

The increase in reports of teen suicides and destructive behaviors occurs in cities, towns, and rural areas. The rate of suicide by young people may have increased by more than 300 percent since 1955. People of every age ask if teen suicide can be prevented. It can be. Every day, more than a thousand young people in the United States attempt suicide. This need not be.

Suicide has recently surpassed homicide as a cause of death for young people, making it the second leading cause. While thousands of children and young people fight bravely against cancer, suicide claims more lives than this dread disease. Some experts claim that up to one in every ten students plans suicide, putting them in a class they call "at risk."

In fact, no one knows the exact number of young people who take their own lives. Many suicides are reported as accidents, or even as murder, sometimes to protect their families and friends from the pain and stigma surrounding suicide. And there are destructive acts, such as taking too many aspirins, or accidents, that are masked acts of self-destruction. Every attempt is a cry for help. We need to see even violent behavior as potentially self-destructive.

Excluding cases where a deranged individual acts against him- or herself or if there is terminal illness, the decision to commit suicide is almost always a combination of a wish to live and a wish to die. This is called "ambivalence." A person who is suicidal usually leaves a message or a trail of signs that hint of his or her intentions. Some of the signs may be subtle, but they can be recognized as a cry for help by someone who knows how to read them.

As many as 70 percent of a large number of people who were questioned in connection with a survey of suicide behavior have indicated that suicide has touched their lives because of the actions of friends and relatives. No wonder so many people want to do something about these tragic and unnecessary deaths.

The following cases of suicide might be reported in the newspapers of almost any large city during almost any month of the year:

> A young celebrity enjoys success but suffers from personal pressures and problems. After spending an evening chatting with friends, he shoots himself in the head with his own pistol.
>
> A young man throws himself in front of a train with the obvious intent of committing suicide. A year later, on the anniversary of the young man's death, a girl who loved him follows the same pattern of action.
>
> A girl's father dies when she is ten years old. For the next few years she is moody. Sometimes she is sad about her father's death. Sometimes she is angry at him because he left her. One night she writes a note saying that she is going to be with her father and she takes an overdose of sleeping pills.

Why do these people take their own lives? Could these deaths have been prevented? Many people have explanations as to what happened and why it happened. The experts are more cautious. They know that suicide is the result of many different and complex factors and that each case is different.

For some people, the subject of suicide contains a certain fascination. For others, the subject is just too horrible to think about. Fortunately, a great many people, perhaps like you, are interested in learning what can be done to help the desperate, lonely, and often confused people who attempt to take their own lives.

There are more questions about suicide than answers. Do people have the right to commit suicide? Do those who feel that they no longer want to live really want to die? How can they be helped? What causes them to choose suicide? Will reading about suicide cause people to take their own lives? You can find the answers to some of these questions as you read later chapters in this book. You can be sure right now that reading about suicide is not one of the causes. In fact, just the opposite may be true. For those people who exhibit self-destructive behavior to a serious degree, becoming aware of their intentions tends to decrease the chances of suicide. Refusing to discuss suicide with a person who is considering it frustrates attempts at communication. Open and honest discussion can be the first step in suicide prevention.

Experts believe that a key factor in the reduction of suicides lies in the spreading of information that can help people tell the difference between the well-established facts and the fallacies. Suicide is a subject steeped in erroneous folklore, superstitions, and myths. Many of the false ideas are dangerous because they prevent the recognition of danger signals.

Suicide need not be America's unspoken tragedy. Knowledge about suicide may save thousands of lives, perhaps even someone you know. You may be the vital link that assures help, professional assistance, for a person who does not really want to die but who can no longer tolerate feelings of hopelessness, helplessness, and emotional isolation. The choice of life is the alternative to suicide. You may help point the way to it.

CHAPTER

2

PATTERNS
OF
SUICIDE

Often one does not know the full circumstances behind a suicide, since each individual is unique. Hostility, anxiety, feelings of inferiority and worthlessness, wanting to cause guilt feelings in others, are just some of the emotions that combine to make people flirt with death. But even though each case is complex, there appear to be common situations that act as triggers for the event. Examining patterns of suicide may help us to recognize danger signals and provide some insight into causes. Have you read about any suicides that seem to fit into the following patterns?

ATTEMPTS TO
MANIPULATE OTHERS

In many cases of suicide, the person tries to manipulate very important or significant people in his or her environment by producing guilt feelings in them. Consider the case of a young boy who desperately wants a car of his own. He has tried all kinds of pleas, threats, and other behavior in efforts to get what he wants, but his parents do not buy the car for him. Since he is being treated by a doctor for his long-term depression, medication is in his bureau drawer. After consulting the doctor about what would or would not be a lethal dose of his medicine under the guise of a friend's wanting to know, the boy takes enough pills to scare his parents. He is gambling with death, but he takes the risk. He believes that his parents will be so sorry when the nearly empty pill bottle is discovered that they will no longer deny him a car. They may think he will really try suicide again if they do not respond to his wish. If his manipulations or attempts at blackmail do not bring the desired results, the above episode may be repeated in a variety of ways. At some point, the boy may actually lose the gamble with death. Or he may reach a therapist who can help him sort out the disturbed feelings that cause him to make unrealistic demands.

While suicide in children is not common, some boys and girls over the age of five do attempt to manipulate parents, or others, in this way. Adults, too, may retain childish behavior and use attempted suicide as a form of manipulation either consciously or unconsciously. For them, too, plans may be upset and an accidental suicide may occur.

MAGICAL THINKING AND ATTEMPTS TO PUNISH

Some magical thinking can be present in the attempt to manipulate others. Another pattern of suicide that involves magical thinking occurs when a person considers suicide as a way to be completely powerful and in complete control. After all, if one cannot feel powerful in any other way, one *can* be master of the way in which one dies. Suicide can be viewed as an omnipotent act. This may seem to be somewhat like burning down a house to get rid of an odor, but for people who are confused, desperate, and/or feeling utterly inferior, here is a way to experience power and to punish those who keep him or her from power in life.

Many children do not realize the finality of death and think that they will be present at their own funerals to enjoy the weeping parents or others who have punished the child in a way that was felt to be unjust. "You'll be sorry when I'm gone" is a frequent taunt of children who are powerless to return punishment. Since they are frustrated, they attempt to take revenge by fantasies of committing suicide. They picture how sorry a parent would be to see them dead and relish the remorse and guilt feelings they have caused. While relatively few children act out such fantasies, some do without realizing that they cannot return to life in some magic way.

Adults who are unable to express hostility in some direct way are more prone to fantasize about, or even attempt, suicide than those who can openly express aggression. An ancient Japanese custom, rarely practiced today, shows this type of suicide quite clearly. A person who had suffered a severe emotional affront, especially from someone of a higher social class who could not be approached directly, might commit suicide on the enemy's doorstep. Many adults of other cultures have taken their lives and carry out apparent wishes to avenge themselves by making another person feel guilty. Although this wish to die may be greater than the desire to live, it often appears to be related to a denial of the finality of death.

THE ANNIVERSARY SUICIDE

An example of the anniversary suicide was mentioned on page 11. The girl who threw herself in front of the train exactly one year after the man she loved had committed suicide this way is just one of many instances in which people attempt to join others who have taken this action. A person may follow the pattern of another by choosing the same day, the same method, or both. About one-third of those who attempt suicide seem to be influenced by the suicide of someone who was close to them. Perhaps the first suicide lowers the second person's restraints against this kind of act.

ACCIDENTAL SUICIDE

Some accidental deaths are expressions of an unconscious death wish. A person may be hemmed in by frustration and desperately lonely but feel prevented from suicide because it is against religious beliefs or considered cowardly. Such a person may seek risks in which death appears to be accidental. For example, a driver who smashes a car into a tree may have driven carelessly because of some unconscious desire to die. A racing car driver may continue to race after having had a number of crashes until one is fatal.

Alcoholics rank high in the statistics of suicide. Some experts believe that the alcohol releases uncontrollable rage or discharge of impulses which results in suicide that often appears to be accidental. Drunken drivers who kill themselves in single car accidents are often considered to have unconscious suicidal wishes.

DRUG ABUSE

A large percentage of young people who commit suicide have been drug abusers before their deaths. This does not necessarily mean that the drugs led to the suicide, but it probably does mean that the same emotional problems or conflicts that led them to drugs played a part in their suicides. Drug abuse may have been a trigger.

IMITATIVE SUICIDES

Although reading about suicide does not appear to increase the amount of this kind of action, suicide in an individual's family does. Since young members of a family imitate certain behavior patterns of parents, or other older relatives, it has been suggested that a person close to someone who commits suicide may always carry the idea that in some way death is a way out of extremely stressful circumstances. The fact that this way was taken by a respected person in the family may increase the chances of its use. It is necessary for the individual to have identified strongly with the deceased.* Other possible reasons that suicides tend to repeat in some families include innate or genetic predisposition to severe depression, family exposure to stresses, guilt and grief that are caused by the first suicide, and/or ways in which families relate. While some families are warm and loving, others are cold and rejecting. Children who grow up with feelings that they are weak and who are unable to cope with their environment are more apt to suffer from despair and use suicide or suicidal behavior as an adaptation.

HOMICIDE-SUICIDE

The idea of aggression turned outward as a cause of murder, and aggression turned inward as a cause of suicide is repeated again and again by experts who have explored the subjects of suicide and death. Karl Menninger, in *Man Against Himself*, describes three types of motivation for all suicides. They are a wish to kill, a wish to be killed, and a wish to die.

*Some who imitate the suicide of a close relative feel that they have been "programmed" to follow the same pattern of behavior and are fated to follow the same script.

Consider the case of a young man who had appeared troubled for a number of years. One winter day, neighbors found him bleeding from stab wounds. He told people that he had been "jumped," but many people believed that the wounds were self-inflicted. About a year and a half later, the twenty-year-old man killed six people as they jogged, walked, or rode motorcycles near a railroad track. The killer dragged each body into the bushes and then waited for the next person to come along. When apprehended by the police, the man committed suicide. Authorities were at a loss to explain the slayings, but those who knew the man at school and in his neighborhood described him as a person who had been troubled for a long time. Here, and in many other cases, aggression turned outward resulted in the murder of others and aggression turned inward resulted in the murder of self. Of course, this does not explain why this person suffered from such aggression or expressed it in the tragic way that he chose.

HEROIC SUICIDES

For some cultures, the act of taking one's life is considered heroic. In previous times, the Japanese military class instilled the idea of the possible need for self-destruction in their children when they were very young. A situation in which honor was involved meant self-destruction without personal choice for the Japanese nobility of olden times. Such suicide, the best-known form of which is hara-kiri, was considered compulsory.

In India, a Hindu widow is forbidden by law to throw herself on the funeral pyre of her husband but at one time this was the custom among women of the upper castes. This practice, known as suttee, was instilled in women from childhood and those who did not commit such heroic suicides lived in shame.

During World War II, Japanese kamikaze pilots flew to certain death for the good of their country. Soldiers far and wide in many wars have died for their ideals in a form of heroic suicide. Idealistic young people have died for many causes, some taking violent action in the cause of nonviolence. For example, Buddhist monks who bathed in gasoline, ignited themselves, and calmly burned to death were performing an act of self-destruction in their effort to communicate their message of protest against violent action.

ROMANTIC SUICIDES

When death is made tragically beautiful in literature, it is a short step for some people to believe that their own deaths may accomplish some romantic meaning. Fortunately, most people identify with a dying hero or heroine in fiction only in their imaginations and live to experience these and other emotions again. For anyone who is troubled and actually identifies with a character to the point of death, no experience of fulfillment survives.

HELPLESSNESS
AND HOPELESSNESS

These are just some of the characteristic patterns of suicide. The common features of helplessness, hopelessness, and emotional isolation appear again and again. The people who commit suicide see their lives as empty of meaning. Those they see as villains and want to punish are destroyed only in the minds of the people who cease to live.

CHAPTER

3

WHY SUICIDE? CONFLICTING THEORIES

Whenever a person commits suicide, people ask why. The patterns of suicide show some of the circumstances that lead to the final act. None fully answers the question, Why suicide? This question has been asked long before people made an attempt to define what constitutes suicide. And it will continue to be asked far into the future.

DEFINITIONS OF SUICIDE

Even the word *suicide* is difficult to define. A common definition is "the act of intentionally destroying oneself." But there are instances in which a suicide occurs but another individual acts as the vehicle. The soldier who throws himself on a grenade to spare others does not fit the usual definition of intentional suicide. Many investigators define suicide as a violent, self-inflicted destructive action resulting in death. Practically all, if not all, medical-legal definitions include the concept of playing a major role in bringing about one's own death.

A recent edition of the Oxford University Press Psychiatric Dictionary defines suicide simply as "the act of killing oneself."

The word *suicide* is a relatively recent one. Although the exact date of its first use is not certain, it was probably introduced about the middle of the seventeenth century. Before that time, people referred to the act as self-murder, self-slaughter, self-destruction, and defined it with such expressions as "to cause violence to oneself," "to fail by one's own hand," "to procure one's own death," and so on.

Even today's professionals and researchers disagree among themselves about basic definitions of such terms as *suicide attempt, suicide gesture, suicidal,* and even *death.* One coroner in the United States is reported to certify death as a suicide only if a note is found. Since the estimated percentage of suicides in which notes are left varies from 10 percent to 40 percent, the number of suicides reported by this coroner is vastly understated. One reason his figures are low may be his concern about the problems that a suicide creates for the family of the victim. Each relative and friend asks why, again and again. Many, like the coroner, want to deny that suicide occurred.

"Andy could not have deliberately jumped in front of that car," insists a mother whose son took his life. She can find no reason why.

"Kim could not have destroyed herself by reckless driving. She was so happy."

"He had so much to live for," is a remark that is commonly heard among those who continue to question why a person committed suicide. Why one and not another?

No one knows really why any person commits suicide and there is no single theory that satisfactorily explains the many possible causes of suicide. The suicidal act has been described as the end of a dark tunnel.

Many people can describe an event, like the straw that broke the camel's back, that precipitated the attempt of suicide. But many others do not know what triggered their attempts. Those who work with large numbers of people who have tried to take their lives admit they are mystified by many of the situations.

Why are some people suicidal while others are not—even when external stresses appear to be equal? Not every deeply depressed person commits suicide. Not everyone who feels helpless and hopeless is self-destructive. And not every self-destructive act can be interpreted as suicidal. Many people who indulge in some form of self-destructive behavior, such as heavy smoking, excessive use of alcohol, or overeating, are not motivated by the wish to die. They are careful with their health otherwise.

The search for a common denominator to suicide has been long and varied. Theories are numerous and many have overlapping features, but most scientific approaches are relatively modern. The earlier theorists were concerned most with the rightness or wrongness of the act rather than the causes.

Certainly, suicide evokes many inconsistent and contradictory feelings. The story of Kitty Jay is just one illustration, but it is a particularly interesting one because of tradition which is carried on to modern times. According to oral history, Kitty Jay was a foundling who lived in the middle of the eighteenth century. She was taken in by owners of one of the great houses on the moor in South Devon, England, and employed as a servant. Here she became romantically involved with one of the sons of the great house. There was no possibility of marriage when she became pregnant because of class distinction. Usually a family helped such a girl financially, but in this particular case, no provision was made. Kitty Jay was to be turned out without the benefit of the care often provided in such situations. Her despair was so great that Kitty Jay went to one of the barns and hanged herself.

Even though there was no question of murder in the case of Kitty Jay, a coroner's jury was called to examine the case. They were to decide whether or not the girl was of sound mind at the time she hanged herself, for this would determine whether or not she could be buried in the churchyard. If she were of sound mind when she took her life, Kitty Jay could not be buried in consecrated ground. Since the jury ruled that this was the case, she was buried according to the custom of the time—at the crossroads where every beggar's foot might pass over her grave.

The attitude of the local people was one of sympathy for this person who had committed suicide. A headstone was placed at the grave and it was surrounded with stones as protection from the footsteps of those who walked at this crossroads on the moors. According to local tradition and folklore, each day someone has placed fresh wild flowers or greens on this grave for more than two centuries. No one suspects ghosts, but no one will tell who places the fresh flowers or greens there. Perhaps it is the ancestors of the family whose illegitimate child died when Kitty Jay committed suicide. Certainly, the attitude of the people in the community differed from the attitude of the jury about a suicide that lives on in the memory of people for such a long time. But neither the people nor the jury really gave the answer to the question, Why suicide?

From the time of Kitty Jay to today, many scientific studies and statistics have explored the question of why people take their own lives.

MORSELLI'S STUDIES

Henry Morselli, an Italian professor of psychological medicine, was an early investigator of the subject. He wrote a book called *Suicide: An Essay on Comparative Moral Statistics*, which was originally published in Milan in 1879 and was reprinted in 1975 by Arno Press in New York. He noted that there were many secret motives that eluded even the suicidal individuals themselves because they acted upon them unconsciously. Morselli explored many statistics and attempted to relate "cosmico-natural" influences (climate, geological formations, and so on), ethnological influences (races, nationalities), biological influences (sex, age), social conditions of the individual (civil status, profession, economic position, social status), and individual psychological influences. While many of Morselli's conclusions would be challenged today, his work was a beginning in the study of a subject that heretofore had been avoided.

In correlating the body stature of people and suicide, Morselli concluded that taller people are more prone to suicide than shorter people. He stated, "With respect to Italy, by comparing the geographical distribution of suicide with that of stature, the following is the formula by which their relation may be expressed: The frequency of suicide in the various parts of Italy generally is in a direct ratio with stature, and the inclination to self-destruction increases from south to north as the stature of the Italians gradually increases."

While many aspects of Morselli's approach seem strange to modern thinking, there is a study in the Spring, 1977 Issue of *Suicide and Life Threatening Behavior: The Official Bulletin of the American Association of Suicidology* that attempts to correlate the number of suicides with the position of the moon. The only significant relationship appeared to be an increase in the suicide rate during the new-moon phase, suggesting that a small percentage of suicide-prone people are affected by lunar changes.

DURKHEIM'S THEORY

Perhaps the most famous research into causes of suicide is Emile Durkheim's classical study. This was first published in French in the year 1897, and it continues to be important reading for any serious student of the subject. Durkheim, who lived from 1858 to 1917, grouped suicides into four basic patterns as follows: egoistic, altruistic, anomic, and fatalistic.

Egoistic suicide results (when a person no longer finds a basis for existence in life) The person feels alienated from society, has too few ties with the community, and is suffering from loneliness and isolation) Most suicides in the United States fall into this group.

Altruistic suicide involves an opposite type of relationship. In some societies, where people are greatly bound and dedicated to a cause, suicide is considered honorable. These are "heroic suicides," such as those of the Japanese kamikaze pilots in World War II or the fiery deaths of Buddhist priests in protest of the Vietnam War.

Anomic suicide is related to great change in a person's family relationship, career, health, or other important aspect of life. The term *anomie* literally means "deregulation." Sudden change for the better may also precipitate suicide. For example, a person who is promoted into a more demanding job may find it too stressful and use suicide as an escape. Or a person who is an Olympic winner may feel there is nothing else to strive for.

Fatalistic suicide occurs among prisoners, slaves, or others in situations of excessive regulation.

These descriptions of Durkheim's categories are overly simplified, but they give one an idea of his approach to the study of suicide. According to Durkheim, the suicide rate is related to the strengths and weaknesses of society. The causes are external or environmentally determined. Suicide is considered a social disease and prevention dependent on social change. His various categories are described in some length in his book and are discussed and criticized in many other books. One of the most important contributions that Durkheim made in the area of suicide was to stimulate further research on the subject.

FREUD'S THEORIES

While Durkheim's theory points to something being wrong with the social situation, Sigmund Freud (1856–1939) viewed suicidal urges as essentially a problem within the individual. Freud believed that life and death forces are in constant conflict in every person, even though these forces are unconscious. Frustrations may cause the aggressive side of the person's emotions to become directed inward. Murdering oneself is considered a way of killing the image of a person who is both loved and hated. In this sense, the suicidal individual identifies with the person he or she unconsciously wants to kill. Freud's studies on suicide were far more extensive than the ideas mentioned here. His theories were developed between the years 1881 and 1939.

Sylvia Plath, the poet and author of *The Bell Jar*, a novel that tells about a personal suicide attempt, lost her father when she was nine. Her poem "Daddy" is a vivid example of an intense struggle with ambivalent feelings about a dead parent. Freud argued that suicide was an outcome of the ego's struggle to cope with loss. Sylvia Plath's identification with the lost father involved mourning which turned inward because of ambivalent feelings of love and hate for her father. The split feelings can be exhausting, as in her case. She wrote in her poem of her desire to be "finally through" with her father and of the "vampire who said he was you." After flirting with death, through several earlier suicide attempts, this brilliant young woman died when a servant failed to enter her gas-filled kitchen at the time she was scheduled to arrive. Sylvia Plath left a note saying, "Please call Dr. _____." His telephone number was included in the note, but it was too late when she was discovered. Her cry for help misfired because the gas drugged the man who lived on the floor beneath her and he could not be awakened to open the door for the servant. This risk-taking activity of Sylvia Plath is a vivid example of Freud's theory of ambivalence toward a lost parent, or love object, and of other theories about unfinished "grief work" in which there is an abnormal desire for reunion with a lost loved one. It is also a good example of the ambivalence of many would-be suicides.

ADLER'S THEORY

Alfred Adler lived from 1870 until 1937 and was considered an important figure in the world of psychology. He was one of the members of a group of psychoanalysts who followed Freud, but he broke away and developed his own concepts. He is most frequently associated with the concept of inferiority complex, and it is through this that he explains his theory of suicide. He describes the suidical person as one who suffers from extreme feelings of inferiority, self-centered goals, and hidden aggression. The person, who is often the product of a pampered childhood, uses suicide as an attempt to manipulate people in an environment in which he or she is unable to relate satisfactorily to others. Adler argues that the suicidal person may see death as a way of proving worthlessness and showing others that he or she is not worth caring for. For some, suicide may offer the increased self-esteem through mastery over life and death.

MENNINGER'S THEORY

Karl Menninger, born in 1893, built his suicide theory on that of Freud. The three main components, a wish to kill, a wish to be killed, and a wish to die, were mentioned in connection with the homicidal-suicidal pattern described briefly on pages 17–18. Freud explained suicide as the winning of the death instinct over the life instinct. Menninger separates suicides into three categories: chronic suicide in which self-destructive behavior is seen, as in addiction, antisocial behavior, martyrdom, and psychosis; organic suicide in which the death wish is the response to a physical illness such as cancer; and focal suicide in which there is self-mutilation and/or multiple accidents. In the book *Man Against Himself*, Menninger examines and analyzes the deeper motives of suicide and the three categories mentioned above. In the final section, he deals with available techniques of combating self-destruction.

HORNEY'S THEORY

Karen Horney (1885–1952) made an outstanding contribution to the field of psychotherapy and her writings include a different approach to explaining people's susceptibility to suicide. She believed that parental attitudes may cause a neurotic dependency in which the child is overcome by feelings of anxiety. When parents are indifferent to the needs of the child, provide a cold family atmosphere, set excessively high standards, or are constantly critical, a child may develop neurotic dependencies characterized by feelings of uneasiness, dread, and impending disaster (basic anxiety). Insecure in a hostile world, the child feels isolated and helpless. Feelings of hostility develop which become so powerful that they cannot be expressed because of helplessness and guilt. The more the hostility is repressed, the more intense the basic anxiety becomes.

One of the ways in which such a child might attempt to overcome the anxiety is to turn hostile feelings inward and to withdraw into a shell to avoid being hurt. Or there may be attempts to compensate for feelings of helplessness by exerting power over others. Feelings of superiority may be substituted for those of inferiority. The child or childlike adult develops an idealized self with a need for affection and approval that can never be satisfied.

In the process of devoting energies in living up to the idealized self (which is unreal), such a person destroys relationships with other people. This could be due to an excessive need for love, an excessive need for power or possessions, or to the feeling that the individual is misunderstood by others. Horney defined these psychological abnormalities as a failure in social and emotional growth. According to her theory, suicide is one type of failure in self-development. As in many other theories, the element of helplessness appears to play an important part.

HENDIN'S STUDIES OF SCANDINAVIA

Dr. Herbert Hendin, a psychoanalyst, made an extensive study of the varying causes of suicide in Denmark, Sweden, and Norway. For a hundred years or more, the rate of suicide in Denmark and Sweden has been three times as great as in Norway. Why?

Dr. Hendin went to Scandinavia where he worked with professionals, patients, and others, and gathered large amounts of data before publishing his findings. He found the differences in the suicide rates to be related to child-rearing patterns.

In Norway, where the rate is comparatively low, children are not required to excel in order to win their mothers' affection. Norwegian adults do not drive themselves toward success or experience self-hate if they fail in their undertakings. Children are reared to express their natural aggression. When there is aggressive antisocial behavior, strong guilt feelings are aroused. In general, one finds suicide only when this aggression is turned inward.

In Sweden, there are rigid demands on children for superior performance and self-hate is associated with failure. In Sweden, suicidal people are identified as "performance types."

In Denmark, the high rate of suicide is thought to be the result of a high degree of dependency. Here a child's dependency on the mother is encouraged far more than in the United States. Aggression is held strictly in check and a behavior pattern develops that increases the amount and length of dependency. When the time for separation from the mother finally comes, it is very difficult because of the intense dependency and feelings of guilt. The Danes have been described as people who are either dependent on someone or on whom someone is dependent. When something goes amiss in this relationship, suicide is a more common answer for people who are under stress than in many other countries.

Of course, the above patterns are not characteristic of every individual, but they do represent a trend. Although Hendin's methods of studying suicide have been criticized and not everyone agrees with his conclusions, this theory sheds some light on what motivates a Danish or a Swedish person to suicide and why the rate of suicide is higher in Denmark and Sweden than in Norway. And it may help in the understanding of the causes of suicide everywhere.

THE CRIMINAL
PERSONALITY THEORY

Samuel Yochelson and Stanton E. Samenow, who are famous for their research at Saint Elizabeth's Hospital, in Washington, D.C., presented an interesting theory of suicide in their famous book, *The Criminal Personality*. According to them, a criminal's thought patterns are based on alternating feelings of worthlessness and omnipotence. In their research of fifteen years, they noted that suicidal thinking occurred from time to time in the life of every criminal they encountered. At such times, the criminal sees himself or herself as worthless and considers life not worth living. The criminal not only sees his or her own life as nothing, but feels that others are aware that this is true, and that the condition will last forever.

The suicidal phase in the life of the criminal is more than a state of depression with anger turned inward. According to this theory, the criminal is angry because his or her needs are not being fulfilled, and current suffering is seen as unending. Feeling that he or she is a victim of circumstances and there is no way out of the present intolerable situation, the criminal sees suicide as a resolution to the pain of lowered self-esteem and the anger that rages against the outside world.

THE CONTAGION THEORY

Examples of cluster suicides, those that occur in the same community within a short period of time, got vast attention in the eighteenth century. Scores of young Germans took their own lives after reading a romantic story of unrequited love, Goethe's *The Sorrows of Young Werther*. Only recently has today's public begun to wake up to a concern that suicides (now much publicized in the media) could provoke more suicides—so-called "cluster suicides." No one believes that suicide is contagious in the same way that measles or colds are contagious. However, we notice something when our attention is drawn to it. Could one suicide have a ripple effect? There is a risk that the news of one suicide might push other young people who dwell on ideas of self-destruction to follow one of their impulses.

When a young person who is popular, good-looking, an outstanding athlete, or has some other enviable quality, commits suicide the act shakes the entire community. People find it difficult to understand the action, making the suicide appear mysterious or glamorous in the eyes of those young people who are troubled. Some, who are already marginal about destructive behavior and desperately want peer acceptance, take their own lives. This is a tragic plea for positive attention, an attempt to enjoy in death the same high status as the first suicide. If there is a domino effect—one suicide seeming to cause classmates and/or friends to acts of self-destruction—it may be partly due to the "romantic" death of the admired peer.

Many younger adolescents who are pulled into a cluster suicide phenomenon may harbor the "magical" or juvenile belief that they are all-powerful and can reverse death, can have death without dying. The horror of death—its ugliness and finality—is denied. An attempt that fails—and most do—can leave a young person scarred or blind or brain-damaged for life.

The suicidal impulse is temporary; it passes. Death and disfigurement are "forever."

MANY THEORIES AND MANY QUESTIONS

Just a few of the theories about why people take their own lives have been mentioned in this chapter. There are many more ideas that have been developed in attempts to help answer the question, Why suicide?

No single theory is very helpful in explaining why one person resorts to suicide and another does not. Each person has a different combination of reasons, but each person probably experiences some of the following feelings: loneliness, hate, shame, guilt, fear, desire for revenge, hopelessness, helplessness, isolation from society, and more. And these feelings, along with others, probably exist in an endless variety of combinations.

The suicidal crisis appears to come most often when the victim feels no hope for the future. Even though there may be many possibilities for a better life situation, these are overlooked, or denied, by the individual. Suicide, rather than being a desire for death, often appears to be more a fear of living and the problems that come with it.

CHAPTER

4

FEELINGS
ABOUT
SUICIDE

Attitudes about suicide have ranged from condemning people to death for trying to take their own lives to a legal defense of the individual's right to choose death. Catholicism and Islam look upon suicide as a sin. At the other extreme, some people feel that someone else should not decide for an individual whether he or she has the right to take his or her own life.

Most doctors and other caretakers make every effort to prevent suicide. They feel that it is their obligation as physicians to point out that how one thinks is influenced by how one feels. Even pain passes. The "decision" to commit suicide should be postponed until treatment for a condition has been completed. In order to protect a suicidal patient, a doctor may advise the family to remove all possibly lethal things from the home until the high-risk period is over. Some individuals have to be hospitalized, even against their will, in order to protect them.

What of those whose treatment cannot bring a cure? Do terminally ill patients have the right to take their own lives? Opinions vary about the right to die, but there are cases where hospitals have permitted some of those patients to choose death.

In some cases, medical personnel refused to allow a terminally ill hospital patient to die. Long legal battles followed. For example, a paraplegic who felt she no longer wanted to live demanded that she be allowed to starve herself, but she could not do this without the cooperation of her hospital. Such cases have been decided by the court. Courts in at least seven states have ruled in favor of a patient's right to refuse medical treatment in the form of life-support systems even at the risk of death.

Is a cancer patient in severe pain who refuses treatment committing suicide? Is a severely burned individual who cannot live more than a week a case of suicide if he or she refuses special care?

Consider the young woman with terminal cancer who is suffering intense pain. She asks her doctor if she is going to die. He admits that he can try to prolong her life by a painful treatment, but she must decide if she wants this. Given the choices of ordinary care, such as painkillers, or maximum effort, the young woman chooses ordinary care. She dies within hours rather than within weeks. Is this suicide? If so, how would feelings about this compare with those about the suicide of a temporarily depressed person who dies by poison?

Consider the case of a young man who is poised, ready to leap from the ledge of a tenth-story window. Do you feel that someone should try to stop him? Does he have the right to take his own life? Would he really want to do this if he lived another twenty-four hours?

In most cases of this type, the impulse to end life is transitory. It may last a few hours, a few days, or be only a momentary feeling. While the wish to die may be repeated, it may be overcome if the person can be given help at the time of the crisis and for a period after that. This is not always the case, however.

The ambivalent nature of suicide is well established.

Even when there is long and involved preparation for suicide, the desire to live is usually present. One who appears very determined to die may actually be experiencing a strong desire to be rescued.

How you feel about rescuing a person or about a person's right to suicide depends partly on the individual situation, but your feeling at any time is probably influenced by attitudes that people have had about this kind of action in the past. Even though the word *suicide* is relatively new, the taking of one's own life has undoubtedly occurred since prehistoric times.

ANCIENT EGYPT

Some of the early records of suicide come from Egypt and indicate varied attitudes toward it. One Egyptian document, dated about 2000 B.C., contains an illustration of a man who might be contemplating suicide, but historians do not agree on the subject matter. According to the interpretation of Jacques Choron, an expert in the study of suicide, the man appears to be tired of life and is trying to persuade his soul to accompany him in death. The soul is afraid that the man will be denied a proper funeral because of the suicide and thus forfeit its chances of a blissful afterlife. Since the ancient Egyptians showed such great concern about life after death, it is not surprising that Choron's interpretation of the Egyptian picture includes this concern with the afterlife.

In a later reference to suicide in early Egyptian literature, a wise man bemoans the state of social decay of the times with the remark, "Death and suicide are common, and the river is filled with corpses."* Suicide was a fairly common fate for condemned criminals in

*L. D. Hankoff, "Ancient Egyptian Attitudes toward Death and Suicide," The Pharos of Alpha Omega Alpha Medical Honor Society, vol. 38, no. 2 (April 1975), pp. 60–64.

Egypt, and history shows there was no prohibition against anyone ending his or her life that way. The most famous Egyptian suicide, of course, was Cleopatra, who, according to legend, took her life with the help of an asp, a venomous snake.

ANCIENT WARRIORS

Many people in far parts of the earth believed violent and self-inflicted death to be a passport to a better life and another world. Since death came at an early age for most of them due to diseases or injuries for which there were no adequate medical remedies, they sacrificed some of their short lives for what they believed to be a better life after death.

Ancient Gauls and early Germanic tribes are described as having no fear of suicide since they believed that being killed in battle or taking one's life ensured happiness in the next world. Valhalla, the paradise of the Vikings, was the hall of those who died by violence. There, a feast of the heroes was presided over by the god Odin, and only those who died violently could take part. While the greatest honor was death in battle, suicide was the second greatest qualification. Odin is said to have died in a ritual suicide. Many men and animals were later hanged on trees in his honor in the holy grove of Uppsala.

PRIMITIVE SOCIETIES

Some African tribes once followed a common custom in which warriors and slaves committed suicide when the tribal king died. They believed if they died this way they would be with him in paradise.

In many primitive hunting and gathering societies, suicide was common because death was preferable to a life with infirmities, but this was not true everywhere.

Anthropologists and others believe suicide was completely unknown in some primitive tribes.

In many societies where personal fulfillment is less important than the well-being of the masses, both good and bad situations are accepted as part of the natural order of things. In such societies, there was and is less stress-related suicide. If good and evil spirits are responsible for the highs and lows in a person's life, then one does not have to suffer from guilt. Today may be controlled by evil spirits, but tomorrow may be different. So there is always hope that the good will come again, and there is less suicide.

In many primitive cultures, suicide was used as an expression of anger and revenge for highly personal motives. In some of the South Sea Islands, suicide is still considered an honorable act.

Imagine a man who was accused of breaking a tribal taboo by another tribal member. He has climbed to the top of a palm tree and declared to the tribe the name of his accuser, then plunged to his death, diving head first toward the ground. This type of suicide for revenge may have been used to accomplish the destruction of his personal enemy, even if it destroyed the person seeking the revenge. (This is also true in modern times in the case of the people who commit suicide because they want parents or other loved ones to suffer.) In some primitive tribes, there is also the belief that the ghost of the dead person will destroy the offender or his family will do so. In some cases, the laws of the tribe demand that the offender commit suicide, too.

SUICIDE BY WIVES

In some societies of long ago, suicide was acceptable when there were "good" reasons. Those reasons hardly would be considered valid in modern times in the Western world. For example, in the Fiji Islands immediately after a tribal chief died his wives rushed to kill themselves, believing that the one who died first would be the chieftain's favorite wife in the spirit world.

Suttee, the ancient Hindu custom, was practiced for a different reason. Here, the wife threw herself on the funeral pyre, or drowned herself in the Ganges, to atone for her husband's sins and open the gates of paradise for him. This practice, which lasted for hundreds of years, was outlawed in 1829, but it died slowly.

GREEK AND
ROMAN ATTITUDES

Greek and Roman attitudes toward suicide varied according to time and place. In one place, there might be legal approval plus the supplying of the poison hemlock for suicide for a person who was suffering from extreme physical or mental anguish. In another place, a magistrate might condone a suicide if the person had what were considered to be admirable reasons, such as avoiding dishonor, patriotic principles, or great grief. However, there was a time in Athens when the body of someone who had committed suicide was buried outside the city limits. The hand of the body was buried separately because it had committed the crime of self-murder.

Drinking poison hemlock is famous as the method of suicide used by Socrates, the Greek philosopher and teacher of Plato. He was more or less forced by the state to die. Reports vary, but he seems to have supported the general philosophy that suicide was wrong except when there were special reasons, such as being ordered by the state, extreme cases of sorrow or poverty, or when one was in disgrace.

Stoics considered suicide as a natural solution to intolerable conditions of life and their philosophy had much influence in the Greek and Roman worlds. Stoics did not feel that suicide was morally right or wrong, but they considered it a reasonable way to end severe, but only severe, suffering.

In Rome, suicide was often regarded in an economic light, especially where soldiers and slaves were concerned. A soldier who killed himself depleted the power of the army, and a slave who committed suicide was an economic loss to the owner. Slaves represented an investment and were sold with a guarantee against physical blemishes, criminal impulses, or a suicidal nature. If a slave committed suicide within six months after purchase, his or her body could be returned to the seller.

Suicide in Rome that was committed to honor country or defend a cause was considered acceptable. Many Roman nobles took their own lives with great dignity and style rather than suffer the dishonor of punishment.

Suicide became quite common in ancient Rome and this type of death was often public and even casual. People in ancient times did not view death with the horror or fear that they do today, and there were many instances of people being killed for the amusement of others. People are even reported to have offered themselves for execution for a sum of money which was to be paid to their heirs. With the decline of the Roman Empire, attitudes toward suicide changed.

HEBREW ATTITUDES

Hebrew prohibitions against suicide go back to the times when the early Egyptians condoned it, to at least two thousand years before the time of Christ. Since Hebrew fundamentalists believe God owns everything, it follows that one's body belongs to Him. But there have been cases in which heroic suicides have been condoned.

For example, in the fortress of Masada on the edge of the desert of Judea which overlooks the Dead Sea, ancient Hebrews carried out a plan of mass suicide. They chose to free themselves by death rather than become Roman slaves. Reports of how the suicide was carried out vary, but there is little question that this was a heroic, mass suicide. If you visit Israel today, you can see this historic site.

In later years, there were many suicides in Nazi concentration camps by people who were waiting to be slaughtered. This may have been an affirmation of the victims' freedom to control their own lives through fixing the time of their death, or the extreme guilt felt by survivors.

CHRISTIAN ATTITUDES

Many early Christians submitted to Roman torture and allowed themselves to be killed as martyrs for their religion. Suicides in this period, whether direct or indirect, were based on the eagerness to do away with the misery of the world in order to experience the joys of immortality. In the fourth century A.D., Saint Augustine spoke out against suicide and the attitude of Christians changed. From then on, suicide was considered a sin on the basis of its being self-murder and in violation of the commandment, "Thou shalt not kill."

Through the years, however, attitudes continued to change. John Donne, the English poet (1573–1631), wrote *Biothanatos*, in which he launched the first full-scale attack against the attitude of the Christian church. He made a plea for charity and understanding. His book, which his son published after Donne's death, revealed that he had contemplated suicide when he was young. Later theologians were less strict about considering suicide as a sin under all circumstances. Although some Christian views today reflect the early thinking about suicide, funeral rites for suicides are often conducted with the assumption that the person was not able to think rationally and was not responsible for the act.

JAPANESE ATTITUDES

Attitudes and customs in Japan have undergone extensive and rapid change in the last few decades. While hara-kiri was forbidden by law as long ago as 1868, it continued to influence later suicides. Hara-kiri, literally translated as "stomach cutting," is done by disembowelment in a solemn and elaborate ceremony. Young boys of the military class were trained from earliest years that they might some day be called upon to play a part in the hara-kiri ceremony, and this early training is believed to have robbed the practice of some of its horrors. Such ceremonial death was honorable for members of the samurai, or military, class. If a samurai warrior fell into disgrace, hara-kiri would blot out the disgrace. Or the ceremony might be performed to show allegiance to a chief. The helper in the ceremony was often a best friend whose function was to assist by cutting off the head after the person had cut deeply into his abdomen in prescribed fashion. The decapitation was an act of mercy which prevented long suffering before death.

The kamikaze pilots who hurtled their planes against enemy warships ended their lives in a different manner but they, too, died in a heroic, ritual suicide. Near the end of World War II, a number of military leaders committed hara-kiri rather than accept surrender. As late as 1970, a famous Japanese author, Yukio Mishima, committed hara-kiri as a plea for the return of old values and traditions in Japan.

The old attitudes toward suicide of the honored and the military class in Japan probably have a large effect on the rate of suicide at the present time, although most suicides today are of the "Western" type. The suicide rate is especially high for young Japanese women when compared with women in the rest of the world. These women are very vulnerable because of social conditions and role conflicts. The traditional Japanese woman was educated to be dominated by parents, husband, husband's parents, and even by male children. If she was rejected or if she was not chosen to be someone's wife, she had little hope of financial and emotional security. In contrast to this, women in many other countries have a greater chance of succeeding as individuals. This was the case in the United States even before the current concern about equal rights. But all hope was lost for a single woman in a traditional Japanese family, and with hopelessness there is a high rate of suicide. The rate in Japan is high for another reason, too. With modernization in Japan, men from remote provinces came in growing numbers to the cities. Their conservative conception of femininity strongly influenced urban attitudes, which had been more liberal. In merchant districts, where women had a higher status, this provided increasing role conflicts for young Japanese women. Although their rate of suicide has declined somewhat recently, it is still high.

Pressure to do well in school is a cause of suicide in many cultures, but it is especially intense in Japan. Even very young children suffer from strong parental pressure for good work in school since competition is great. Being admitted to a good university means future security and comfort for males and a better marriage for females. Since suicide can be called aggression turned inward, it may not surprise us to find a great number of suicides in a country such as Japan. Expressions of anger toward authority figures are frowned upon. But most Japanese young people do not use suicide as a "valve" to release anger. They find culturally acceptable ways to express their feelings.

IN THE UNITED STATES

The right to die is a much debated question in the United States today. Allowing people to refuse special life-support systems when they are terminally ill has gained increasing support. But what of the person who is attempting to jump from the Golden Gate Bridge?

At one time a vote was taken in the San Francisco area about whether or not an expensive, view-destroying guard rail should be erected on the Golden Gate Bridge to prevent suicides in that popular location. The vote was seven to one against it. Some people may have objected to the cost. Others may have objected to spoiling the view. Some may have objected to the idea of interfering with a person who wants to commit suicide. Or many people may have had mixed feelings. The city of San Francisco has an outstanding suicide-prevention center which receives thousands of calls each year.

Even those who treat suicidal persons do not always agree about the right to commit suicide. According to psychiatrist Dr. Jerome A. Motto of the University of California School of Medicine in San Francisco, suicidal impulses emerge in people who suffer severe pain, whether from physical or emotional sources. Suicide is a way of coping with that pain. Motto feels the problem is not whether or not the patient has the *right* to suicide, but the dilemma that stems from the fact that he or she does have such a right. To what extent should the exercise of that right be subject to limitations?

While a person may have a right to suicide, is the act based on a realistic assessment of the life situation or on a gross distortion? When people are suicidal, they have a distorted view of their lives. A person who feels unworthy, unlovable, and isolated from other human beings may develop a new and more realistic perception through therapy.

Those who would further limit the right to suicide point to the ambivalence of many suicidal people as a kind of self-imposed, if unconscious, limitation of that right. If someone with suicidal impulses is consulting a psychiatrist in the office, calling on the phone, or writing to the doctor, ambivalence is present, for these are ways of calling attention to such impulses. The same applies to contact with a suicide-prevention agency, a hospital emergency room, a hotline, or other helping agency. While these services may or may not be able to fulfill the needs of a person in suicidal crisis, there is a good chance that they may help the person temporarily. Those who claim that a person has a right to suicide must consider the fact that these helping agencies often are called upon at a time when a person is suffering from tunnel vision or disorientation of a temporary nature.

The girl who takes an overdose of sleeping pills and calls the crisis hotline is certainly ambivalent. She may have a right to take her own life, but she may not *really* want to do so. Any expression of ambivalence is a clear indication of resistance to suicidal impulses and, therefore, a limitation of the right to suicide, according to Dr. Motto and many others who have carefully studied this area.

According to some philosophies, people should have the right to do what they wish with their own bodies. A relatively small number of people object to the attitude that those attempting suicide should be rescued. They claim that the central question is who owns the human body, and according to them that owner is the individual, not God or a doctor.

Attitudes about whether or not one has the right to suicide often include some qualifications. As mentioned on page 35, a prevailing attitude at the present time is justification for suicide, or "pulling the plug," in the cases where individuals are suffering from terminal cancer or other serious and fatal illnesses in which there is no chance of recovery. But in cases where there may be hope for better situations in the future, most people feel that suicide should be prevented.

CHAPTER

5

SUICIDE LORE

Suppose one of your friends confides in you that he or she is going to commit suicide. What would you do? What would you say? You might suggest that the friend think of more pleasant things. You might laugh about the remark, hoping that the threat was a joke. You might think that the person is using this threat as a way of getting attention or of manipulating you to do something that you did not plan to do. You might even ignore the remark because you have heard that people who talk about committing suicide never do.

The idea that people who talk about suicide never take their lives is a very dangerous fallacy and one of the most popular parts of the great body of suicide lore. If a friend confides in you that he or she is going to commit suicide, one of the best things you can do is to know the difference between fallacies and truths and act immediately. How to act is described in a later chapter. First, here are some popular fallacies that lead people to wrong responses.

"PEOPLE WHO TALK ABOUT SUICIDE DON'T TAKE THEIR LIVES"

Verbal expressions such as "I might as well be dead" or "You'll be better off without me" are chief among the danger signals or clues given by people who eventually commit suicide. Of 134 families interviewed in a study to determine suicidal communication, it was discovered that 41 percent of the victims had specifically stated their intent to commit suicide. Many investigators report a wide range of verbal clues recalled by families of people who have taken their lives. Since such clues are things most families of victims do not want to remember, it may be that far more victims have given verbal hints about their intentions. Families of suicidal people frequently suffer from feelings of guilt and may forget such statements. Many studies indicate that as many as 60 to 80 percent of the persons who commit suicide had communicated their intentions before they died.

"ALL PEOPLE WHO COMMIT SUICIDE ARE CRAZY"

"Crazy" and "insane" are words we all use, applied mostly to people who behave in ways that seem strange to us. They are also used to label those who are suffering from serious emotional illnesses that affect their behavior. Psychiatrists may use the term "psychotic" to denote a great loss in a person's ability to evaluate his or her perceptions correctly. For example, if an individual thinks that he is receiving messages through his television set, he would be considered to have impaired reality testing. A depressed person who thinks he is possessed by devils who want him to set himself on fire is another example of a severe inability to test reality.

Psychosis may be caused by schizophrenia, drug abuse, alcohol abuse, or other disorders. Some people who are suffering from psychotic disorders may take their lives because their perceptions are severely distorted. For example, a schizophrenic woman heard her dead mother calling, so she overdosed on sleeping pills in order to join her mother in heaven.

"IMPROVEMENT OF A SUICIDAL PATIENT MEANS THE DANGER IS OVER"

Most schizophrenics do not ordinarily commit suicide in response to hallucinations or panic, but those who take their own lives do so because they are unable to adapt when they are in an improved state. In cases of depressive illness, suicide is more likely to occur when the person is improving. S. A. Applebaum has described suicide as a problem-solving technique to "save the integrity of the psychological system despite its catastrophic effects in other respects."[*]

Even after an unsuccessful suicide attempt, one must continue to assess the risk of another attempt. Most suicides happen within three months after the beginning of improvement. The act of suicide usually involves some planning and activity. People who are severely depressed frequently suffer from inertia. When they begin to improve, they have more energy which can be used to put morbid thoughts and feelings into action. It may also be true that improvement is only on the surface, while deep inside the suicidal people are

[*] S. A. Applebaum, "The Problem-Solving Aspect of Suicide," *J. Project. Techn.*, vol. 27 (1963), p. 259.

not really better. Certain people grow calm and appear happy just before suicide because they are no longer in conflict over whether or not to live.

"SUICIDE IS A DISEASE"

Avery D. Weisman made a study at Massachusetts General Hospital, in Boston, on the subject of suicide as a disease.* He concluded that suicide is neither a moral dilemma nor a mental disease, but a form of life-threatening behavior which resembles a declaration of war. There is no evidence of organic disease to explain it, and while disease involves sickness, sickness does not always involve disease. Weisman found that suicide might be an attempt to break through indecision about living and dying, but unfortunately, one may die of the side effects.

Rather than considering suicide as a disease, a crisis, or a conflict, Weisman decided that the sickness of suicide might better be thought of as "lethality." This concept, attributed to the suicidologist Edwin Shneidman, may be broadly defined as the disposition to kill oneself or put one's life in danger. Suicidologists consider lethality as a very helpful concept.

The following case, which illustrates a lethal but no longer suicidal situation, may help to show how these words are used by experts. For several weeks, Ms. X had considered suicide because of family problems that she believed were insurmountable. One day she wrote a suicide note, then she got into her car and drove to a high bridge for a rehearsal of her suicide plans. On the morning of her attempt, she went about her household chores as usual, then drove to the bridge. After parking her car, she climbed over the railing and paused,

* Avery D. Weisman, "Is Suicide a Disease?" *Life Threatening Behavior*, vol. 1, no. 4 (Winter 1971), pp. 219–31.

ready to leap. Again, as she had many times during the past few weeks, she grew undecided about whether or not to end her life. She considered the stigma on her children that would result from her act, but she felt that killing herself was a form of revenge upon her husband. Ms. X believed that people who jumped from high places died before they reached the ground or the water and she expected this to happen to her. She let go of the railing as a way of overcoming her indecision, and fell toward the water. On the way down, she realized she was not dead and wished that she would be rescued. This is known because she *was* rescued by a fisherman who happened to be nearby. After reaching the hospital, she was no longer suicidal; her feelings had changed. No one who helped her while she recovered from her fractures could determine why she suffered from the desire to take her life before her suicide attempt. Conditions at home were no better when she returned but she had broken through her lethality. The suicide attempt may have been partially motivated by guilt and was her way of punishing herself for her imagined faults. In this way she atoned, and thus alleviated her guilt.

Some suicidologists think that the significance of attempting suicide is its use in overcoming the quandary of not being able to choose whether to live or die. The attempt at suicide may be the way used to break through the lethality. Unfortunately, in successful attempts, the cure results in death.

"THE CHANCES OF SUICIDE CAN BE REDUCED BY AVOIDING THE SUBJECT"

Actually, one can reduce the chances of suicide by bringing the subject into the open. If a boy suggests he might kill himself and you respond by saying, "You wouldn't do anything that stupid," you are confirming his already low opinion of himself. He feels more alone, he feels wrong, and he feels even less acceptable than he did before he made the remark that was actually a cry for help.

Since what you say to a suicidal person may play a large part in the life or death of another person, you can see how important it is to know what to say or what not to say. Knowing not to treat suicide as a taboo subject is one of the first steps toward prevention.

The old attitude of hiding or denying suicide has been the cause of many unnecessary deaths. Here is a case in point. A doctor who was treating a young boy for depression and who found him to be suicidal recommended that the boy be hospitalized. He found that the boy's father was cooperative, but the mother would not consider such a thing. What would the neighbors think? She refused to accept the idea that the boy might take his life.

One afternoon, the boy sat in a rented hotel room for three hours with a pistol pointed at his head. Then he put the pistol in his pocket and returned home. Even after the therapist revealed this event to the father, the parents would not consider hospitalization. A few weeks later, the boy threatened to punish his mother for always nagging at him. He hanged himself in the basement while she was getting dinner.

Now, the mother was furious with the doctor for not warning of the possibility of suicide. Both parents visited the doctor and reproached him with angry words and threats. When in the presence of the mother, the father denied ever having been warned of the possibility of suicide. Perhaps they would have to live with feelings of guilt and the stigma of suicide for the rest of their lives. Was this stigma a major part of their grief? How different this case might have been if the parents could have accepted the boy's behavior without their personal concern for the attitudes of others!

Talking about suicide with a person who is trained to help can often minimize the anxiety that goes with this kind of thinking and may prevent the action from taking place. If you recognize a clue to suicide in someone, pick up the phone and get a suicide-prevention center or other emergency center to help him or her.

"SUICIDAL PERSONS AVOID MEDICAL HELP"

A common misconception about suicidal persons is that they shy away from medical help. Studies on the backgrounds of people who have committed suicide show that as many as 60 to 70 percent had sought medical help within six months before the suicide. No one knows exactly how many gave clues to the doctors about their suicide plans, but doctors are becoming more alert to suicidal intent and taking action that can help prevent suicide. The relationship between physical and emotional health is recognized in the work of an increasing number of professionals.

"THERE IS A TYPE OF PERSON WHO COMMITS SUICIDE"

"She was not the type."

"Only the rich commit suicide."

"No wonder he took his life. Suicide is the curse of the poor."

There is no "type" where suicide is concerned. All kinds of people end their own lives. Male and female; young, old, and all the ages in between; rich, poor, and middle-income people; people of all shades of skin; manic and depressive; mentally ill and mentally healthy;

these are all people who have been suicidal. Anyone might be.

So often one hears the statement, "He just wasn't the type," soon after a suicide. Knowing that there is no one type, that any person may be vulnerable may make it easier to recognize clues and prevent the tragic waste of lives through suicide.

"SUICIDE ATTEMPTS
ARE SELDOM REPEATED"

The truth is that once a person tries death by suicide he or she is very likely to make another attempt. Some people make many attempts and continue until they are finally successful.

In determining the risk of suicide, one of the important factors is whether or not the person has attempted suicide before. However, since the suicidal mood is usually a temporary one, a great many people who attempt suicide are diverted from this kind of action and never try again. Even those who try several times may resolve their problems in more positive ways and go on to lead rewarding lives.

"NOTHING CAN BE DONE
ABOUT SUICIDE"

In spite of modern attitudes, many people believe that nothing can be done about suicide. Certainly there are cases where suicide attempts have been stopped and the person commits suicide at a later date. No statistics can ever be available for the actual number of suicides that have been prevented by calls to suicide-prevention centers, but there are hundreds of these centers functioning and an untold number of people who are alive today because of them.

"DECEMBER IS THE MONTH THAT HAS THE HIGHEST RATE OF SUICIDES BECAUSE THERE IS A RASH OF SUICIDE AROUND CHRISTMAS TIME"

Actually, December may have the lowest suicide rate of any month, even though many troubled people feel more depressed just before the holidays. Homicides do increase in some states. Perhaps the Christmas season brings certain stresses, but it increases the sense of belonging to a family or group—even to the whole community—because of good feelings, even with strangers. April has the highest suicide rate, perhaps because people give up on hopes that things may get better when their depression does not lift as spring comes.

"THERE IS LITTLE RELATIONSHIP BETWEEN ALCOHOLISM AND SUICIDE"

Alcohol can increase impulsiveness, depressive feelings, and poor judgment. Although some people believe that adolescents can "drown their sorrows in drink," and so will not take their own lives, alcoholism and suicide often go hand in hand. A report of a National Institute of Mental Health Conference said that 80 percent of adolescents drink alcohol when they attempt suicide. Some people who normally do not turn to alcohol when they feel depressed drink alcoholic beverages just before they take their lives. Young adults tend to retain some traces of magical thinking about the permanence of death. This mistaken notion, taken with alcohol, can be deadly.

"SUICIDE IS A SPONTANEOUS ACT. IT HAPPENS WITHOUT WARNING"

Most suicidal people fantasize or plan their self-destruction long before making the attempt. They give numerous clues and warnings, as mentioned elsewhere in this book. It should be pointed out that when suicides are prevented the majority of people never try it again. They go on to lead full and happier lives, never giving suicide even a passing thought.

CHAPTER

6

SUICIDE NOTES

At first glance, suicide notes might be considered windows into the minds of people who are about to commit suicide. Statistics telling what percentage of people leave notes vary from 20 percent to 80 percent, but large numbers of notes do exist. How such notes are interpreted varies a great deal, too.

Certainly, in most cases suicide appears to be a dramatic detail in a series of circumstances, but the suicide notes are almost always written just before the act. This appears to be one of the reasons that the notes are disappointing to those who hope they will provide insight into the past characteristics of the person. Such notes normally do not expose the real causes of the suicide, even if they do identify the precipitating event.

One famous suicide note that gave some information about the feelings and reasons for suicide was that written by Virginia Woolf to her husband, Leonard. The celebrated British novelist committed suicide by drowning in 1941. The note read:

I feel certain I am going mad again. . . . And I shan't recover this time. I begin to hear voices, and I can't concentrate. . . . I can't fight any longer. . . . What I want to say is I owe all the happiness of my life to you. I can't go on spoiling your life any longer.

TYPICAL EXPRESSIONS IN SUICIDE NOTES

Many suicide notes contain such sentences as: "I am in pain," "I am sorry," "I hate to let you down, this way is best," "Take care of our son and daughter," "Children, be good to your mother [or father]," "You drove me to this," "The car engine needs tuning," "Give Tom the $150 which I owe him," "I hope this is what you wanted," "Be sure to feed my cat."

These messages show some of the things that seem important to people in the final moments of life. Many notes contain just a few sentences. Hostility is often expressed in a disguised way. For example, a note that says, "I'm no good. Mary deserves much better," sounds humble but it may really express hidden hostility. The underlying meaning may be, "Mary makes me feel I'm no good. She thinks she deserves better." While the person may be aware only of the unhappiness that he or she feels, the element of aggressiveness or hostility is frequently expressed. "Mary, I hate you, Love, John" is not uncommon in its combination of sentiments.

Apologies for causing trouble, directions for disposing of one's body, expressions that beg forgiveness, information that indicates the person has given clues of intentions which were ignored are all common elements in notes. Apologies are typical in cases of feelings of low self-esteem, and low esteem is typical in suicidal people. It is not surprising to find notes that include such expressions. One rather famous note was written by a workman who chalked the following on the outside of an abandoned house before hanging himself. He wrote: "Sorry about this. There's a corpse in here. Inform police."

While most suicide notes are found near the body of the writer, a few find their way into newspaper columns that give personal advice. Recently, a writer began a letter to a columnist with an announcement that "this is a suicide note." Then the person, who signed it "No Name, No City, But I've Got Counterparts All Over," proceeded to tell the columnist that she would probably have the same reaction about suicide as most people and stop reading at the beginning of the note. Of course, if the writer had been truly convinced that it was futile to expect help, he or she probably would not have taken the trouble to write.

TUNNEL VISION

People who are about to take their lives are believed to suffer from a condition known as tunnel vision. This is a state in which a person's perception is narrowed and only one alternative, suicide, seems to be the way to cope with problems. In other words, the crisis situation precludes the awareness of other ways to change a situation and stops the person from pursuing a course that will lead out of this suicidal state. Feelings of hopelessness, helplessness, and emotional isolation may be increased by a person's inability to escape from what has been called the "closed world of suicide."

Tunnel vision makes it difficult for anyone to write a note with any depth. Edwin S. Shneidman, professor of thanatology at the University of California at Los Angeles and one of the world's outstanding authorities on suicide, has studied suicide notes for many years. Professor Shneidman wonders if the personal emptiness which may precede suicide might not account for the. fact that suicide notes are relatively arid and psychologically barren.

REAL VERSUS
SIMULATED NOTES

In *Clues to Suicide*, an investigation edited by Edwin S. Shneidman and Norman L. Farberow, there is an appendix which includes over thirty paired suicide notes. One of each pair is a genuine note and one is simulated. The actual notes were obtained from the public records of the coroner's office in Los Angeles County, California, and the other notes were obtained as part of an experiment. Nonsuicidal individuals were asked to write "suicide notes" of the kind they thought they would write if they were going to take their own lives. The nonsuicidal individuals who participated in the experiment were chosen to match, as nearly as possible, many characteristics of the actual note writers. The readers of *Clues to Suicide* can examine the paired notes and test themselves on their ability to distinguish the real from the simulated notes. A key is given at the end. Many people who have read the book or who are knowledgeable about suicide can easily distinguish the real notes from the false ones.

While some actual suicide notes are long, many are short and superficial. Professor Shneidman has said, in his book *Suicidology: Contemporary Developments*, that a truly suicidal person cannot write a meaningful suicide note. Conversely, if one could write a meaningful suicide note that person would not have to commit suicide. The sense of personal emptiness is often expressed as, "I can't find my place in life."

WILLINGNESS TO ANSWER
THE CRY FOR HELP

One suicide note begins with the remark that the stigma suicide brings upon the family "cannot be more than has already been done." In some cases, the very fact that the person feels that stigma may be attached to suicide may be a way of punishing those who the suicidal person believes have treated him or her unfairly.

Even though suicidal people often feel that the stigma attached to suicide is so great that no one will want to help, the numerous suicide-prevention centers throughout the world show the opposite to be true. One interesting experiment in which a person published a suicide note for the reaction it would bring is described in *Life-Threatening Behavior*.* Leland Moss was a student of Professor Edwin Shneidman when this suicidologist was teaching a course in social relations at Harvard University. Mr. Moss placed an ad in the Personals column of the paper *Boston After Dark* which read:

> M 21 student gives self 3 weeks before popping pills for suicide. If you know any good reasons why I shouldn't, please write Box D-673.

The response was surprising, even to the writer of the false suicide note. Within a month, he had received 169 letters, although not all were serious replies by people who cared. Over a third of the responses were received in the first three days after the appearance of the ad. One letter, which came from as far away as Brazil, was written by a minister who was the father of a student at Massachusetts Institute of Technology. The student sent the ad to his father since he felt his father could give good advice.

While many letters told about the writers' own problems, a large number of people suggested ways of coping by developing an appreciation of nature. A large percentage of people who answered did so with com-

---

* Leland Moss, "Help Wanted: A Limited Study of Responses to One Person's Cry for Help," *Life-Threatening Behavior*, vol. 1, no. 1 (Spring 1971), pp. 55–66.

passion and concern. A small group who responded questioned whether or not the ad was sincere, and one remarked, "At first I wondered if you were serious or not. . . . if it's a joke, it's in poor taste . . ."

Such an ad would indeed have been a bad joke if it were done frivolously. But the study of responses told something about people's reactions to suicide notes.

Mr. Moss felt that a sizable number of people who replied to his ad agreed with Professor Shneidman's doctrine that all suicides might be prevented and that a cry for help should be answered as directly and swiftly as possible.

SUICIDAL THINKING PATTERNS

A number of serious studies have been made on suicide notes in efforts to discover more about what goes on in the minds of people who commit suicide. In addition to the authorities already mentioned, others such as Jerry Jacobs, Jacob Tuckman, Gene Lester, David Lester, C. Osgood, and E. G. Walker have analyzed genuine suicide notes and compared them with counterfeit notes. They found that, in general, the real suicide notes contained more words such as "maybe," "but," and "except," indicating that there was increased vacillation in the thinking of suicidal people. Osgood and Walker found a greater number of verbs dealing with simple action in the true notes than in the false ones, and a less frequent use of verbs that dealt with planning and judgment. True notes included many terms of endearment. The studies indicated that one of the hallmarks of suicidal thinking was the inability to reflect on or think through the implications of their thoughts. Conclusions from these and other studies of suicide notes are that people about to commit suicide are rigid, constricted, and polarized in their thinking processes so that they are unable to imagine other ways to cope with problems. Some authorities describe this as an "impoverishment of internal judgment process." It might also be described simply as a type of thinking that ignores other ways out.

Studies of suicide notes may not reveal the nature and causes of suicide, but they do help in understanding the thought processes of the individual about to take his or her own life. Notes do show the pattern of thinking to be a sterile one. Except in cases of terminal illness, the situation appears to be a crisis in which intervention may prevent suicide and give hope for a better future.

CHAPTER

7

TROUBLED MINDS

What are the feelings and thoughts that might lead people to kill themselves? The motivation is different for each individual, but often the forerunner of suicide is the psychic pain associated with depression and other troubled emotional states.

DEPRESSION

Recent surveys tell of an increase in the number of children and adolescents who suffer from severe types of "lows" or depression. Yale University researcher Dr. Myrna M. Weissman says the relatives of people who experienced depression when they were young are far more likely to be depressed, too. Even though it is hard to find a set of rules acceptable to psychiatrists for diagnosing childhood depression, it appears to be increasing.

Everyone has the "blues" occasionally—times when nothing seems right, and when life does not seem to be as enjoyable as usual. The reason may be a let-down feeling after an exciting vacation, a long stretch of bleak weather, or a disappointing event. These are examples of a normal type of depression—a temporarily lowered mood state which does not interfere seriously with one's perception of life or ability to function. Most people manage to recover quickly from minor setbacks, but others stay depressed and cannot overcome their low spirits.

RECOGNIZING DEPRESSION

The risk of a depressed person committing suicide is fifty times higher than for a person who is not depressed. If you can learn to recognize the signs of depression, you may be able to save someone you know from suffering, or even from suicide.

A depressed person may exhibit any of the numerous warning signals in varying degrees. The prevailing mood is that of sadness, and the person may appear gloomy and apathetic. He or she may express feelings of emptiness and numbness, and a lack of ability to enjoy anything. His or her attitude may be hopeless and pessimistic. Feelings of worthlessness, guilt, and anxiety are common. Suicidal preoccupation is often present. There may be difficulty in concentrating or remembering things. Often, the person has trouble making decisions, even concerning unimportant matters.

Friends may notice that the individual has become withdrawn and uncommunicative, and is avoiding social activities that were formerly enjoyed. There is a decline in sexual drive.

Insomnia and other changes in sleep habits are common. Many depressed people awaken very early in the morning and cannot fall asleep again. Others sleep more than usual, thus escaping, at least temporarily, from their emotional pain.

Physical symptoms such as fatigue and loss of appetite are not unusual. In fact, many people who consult physicians for physical complaints such as headaches, palpitations, back pain, and other ailments turn out to be suffering from depression in disguise, or masked depression. Underlying depression may also masquerade as an alcohol problem, compulsive overeating, or sexual promiscuity.

Depression in children and adolescents is often masked, with the result that their behavior is puzzling. When ten-year-old Robert's parents were divorced, his grades began to slip; his teacher complained that he was inattentive in class and picked fights with other children. Robert did not suddenly become a "bad" child. He was reacting to his father's absence.

Depression in children and adolescents often goes unrecognized because the symptoms are deceptive, as in the case of Robert. Other behavior, such as truancy, disobedience, and self-destructive acts may also be expressions of unrecognized depression. Sometimes adolescent depression is not noticed because it is normal for adolescents to experience some extreme fluctuations in mood.

Recent reports in medical journals show that adolescents can often suffer from the same outward and inward signs of depression that adults experience.

Dr. Carl P. Malmquist of the University of Minnesota has noted several warning signs which may be useful clues to depression in children.

1. Persistent sadness, in contrast to the temporary unhappy moods that normally occur in all children from time to time.

2. Low self-concept.

3. Provocative, aggressive behavior, or other behavior that leads people to reject or avoid the child.

4. Proneness to be disappointed easily when things do not go exactly as planned.

5. Physical complaints such as headaches, stomachaches, sleep problems, or fatigue, similar to those experienced by depressed adults.

BIOLOGICAL FACTORS

No one today believes, as the ancients thought, that depression is caused by an excess of black bile in the body. However, we know that the old theories were not totally erroneous. Scientists have discovered biochemical abnormalities in association with depressive states, and they think that these changes in body chemistry may play an important role in the development of depression, or may be the product of depression. Biochemical abnormality is only one of many variables that may be responsible for depression. There is also evidence that genetic factors may play a part in increasing a person's vulnerability to depression.

EXPERIENCE OF LOSS

There have been many studies that suggest there is a definite relationship between emotional loss in the young and the development of depression.

In one experiment, infant monkeys were separated from their mothers and left without any stimulation for forty-five days. When they were removed from isolation, they did not play with the other monkeys, but remained apathetic and huddled in a corner, exhibiting what appeared to be depressed behavior.

Other experiments with monkeys have demonstrated that even short periods of separation from the mother have had long-term effects such as increased clinging to the mother and arrested social development.

Human babies separated from their mothers react in similar fashion. René A. Spitz was one of the first to describe the response of babies as young as six months to the loss of their mothers. A type of depression known as hospitalism used to be seen in institutions, where children did not receive enough mothering from anyone. Even though they were well cared for and all their physical needs met, many of these children became apathetic and withdrawn. Some literally wasted away and died from lack of mothering.

The following case graphically demonstrates the effect of separation and inadequate mothering on a young child. Jimmy was one year old when his mother died suddenly. Until then, he had been a happy, bright, alert child. After his mother's death he was cared for by a succession of housekeepers, none of whom stayed more than three months. He became withdrawn, lethargic, and sad; he stopped smiling and talking. By the age of two years, he looked like a retarded child.

Animal studies and observation of young children have led to the conclusion that early loss or deprivation can make people more sensitized to loss and susceptible to depression in later life. The loss may be actual physical separation, or it may be emotional. Emotional loss may encompass a range of different kinds of emotional rejection by the people taking care of the child, from outright abuse to subtle and hidden hostility.

In adults, loss may be real, fantasized, or symbolic. Examples of real loss are the death of a parent or other loved one, loss of health due to injury or age, loss of status, loss of self-esteem or self-confidence, and loss of security. A fantasized loss involves the loss of hope of fulfilling an important goal in one's life. For instance, Bill broke his leg, thereby preventing him from competing in the Olympics. Although the injury would not prevent him from skiing again, it was severe enough so that it dashed his hopes of entering the Olympics.

He took his life. Most people would not react to this misfortune by committing suicide as Bill did, because most people would not invest so much emotional energy in a single goal.

A young woman lost an inexpensive ring given to her as a child by her mother, who had died shortly afterward. She suffered a depressive reaction to the loss that was not commensurate with the actual value of the ring. It is clear that the ring had symbolic, and not real, value.

No one knows the exact relationship between loss and depression. Each individual is different, and no two people have had exactly similar life experiences. Therefore, each may react differently to the same loss. One may become mildly discouraged, another may become severely depressed, and someone else might commit suicide.

Everyone normally experiences separations and losses throughout life. It has been noted that some people seem better able to overcome loss than others; those who are unable to master these experiences are perhaps more prone to later depression.

STRESS

Investigators studying the effects of stressful life events have found that experiences of loss are high on the list of stressful situations. Dr. Eugene S. Paykel, a British psychiatrist, has analyzed the relationship between life stress, depression, and suicide. For these studies, a list of life situations that are considered stressful was compiled. Examples of some of the thirty-three events are marital separation, serious illness, death of a close family member, a move, marriage, pregnancy, leaving school, change in work, promotion, and being fired. You may be surprised to see that both desirable and undesirable events are included.

Depressed people were shown to have experienced many more of these events than the general population. While there was no significant difference in the number of desirable events, the depressive group reported a much higher incidence of undesirable events than the control group.

Events were also categorized in terms of entrances and exits, that is, the introduction of new people or the departure of familiar people from the individual's life. It was found the depressives reported more exits than did the control group. The exit or departure of an important person from one's life is a loss, and as noted earlier, loss bears an important relationship to depression.

Suicide attempters were compared with depressives and with a control group. The suicidal group reported more events in all categories, except desirable events, when compared with the control group. They experienced the same number of exits as the depressives, but reported a significantly higher number of entrances than either the depressive or the control groups.

The suicidal group was found to have experienced a greater number of events that are designated as threatening. Threatening events include major stressful situations, undesirable experiences, and those situations that are not under the control of the individual. Dr. Paykel's conclusion is that suicide attempts seem to be a response to many different kinds of events, especially those in the threatening category.

When the time of occurrence was studied, it was found that depressive individuals reported a rise in the number of stressful events during the three months preceding relapse of depression. The suicidal group experienced not only a greater number of stressful events during the six months before the attempt, when compared to the general population, but also a significant peak in the month immediately prior to the attempt.

Life stress has been linked with a number of disorders, but no one knows why stress may precipitate depression in one person and suicide in another, while yet another may develop schizophrenia, and others have no significant reaction. Genetic and biological differences, in addition to other unknowns, all play a role in determining the individual's reaction to stress.

HELPLESSNESS, HOPELESSNESS, AND EMOTIONAL ISOLATION

Emotional loss early in life means more than loss of love; it involves the lack of opportunity to interact and elicit responses from a caring person. According to some experts, individuals who discover early in life that no one responds to their needs learn to see themselves as helpless. This learned helplessness may be a significant forerunner of depression. Those who grow up feeling that nothing they say or do has much impact on the world around them are likely to conclude that they have little control over their lives. They begin to see themselves as ineffective and may develop a negative self-image. This negative view leads them to believe that they are more helpless and less competent than they actually are. People who have these kinds of feelings are probably more prone to depression and perhaps more likely to be susceptible to stress in the form of uncontrollable events.

Many researchers have emphasized the importance of feelings of hopelessness as part of depression. In a study of the attitudes of prisoners, investigators found that some prisoners were apathetic and depressed, while others, with equally long sentences, were relatively happy, productive, and interested in many things. Their attitudes were not dependent on the length of sentence, the kind of job they held, or on their treatment by the guards. Their state of mind seemed to be correlated instead with their attitudes about the past and the future. Those who did "hard time" felt pessimistic and hopeless; they had no families or friends outside, no job prospects, did not believe they would be paroled, and thought their sentences were unjust. On the other hand, those who were doing "good time" had a more hopeful and optimistic attitude toward life; they thought their sentences were just, they expected parole, and they had relatives and friends outside. The hopeless, helpless, and emotionally isolated prisoners became depressed, while the others who had a more positive view of life were able to adjust to their unpleasant situation and make the best of it.

Hopelessness has been singled out as a tell-tale sign of high risk among people who are thinking about suicide. In 1985, a team under the direction of Dr. Aaron Beck reported the results of a study in the *American Journal of Psychiatry* that tried to help caretakers identify people who are at high risk. The team intently studied 207 patients who had been hospitalized because of intentions to commit suicide. These patients were followed over a period of from five to ten years. Checks with family and friends, scanning of daily death notices, and, in some instances, following the patients' moves to foreign countries helped the researchers. They found that a high score on the hopelessness test (see pages 73–74) indicated the need for careful observation of a person under treatment for years after leaving psychiatric care. Of the handful who did eventually kill themselves, no predictor, such as a test, forecast their end.

The "hopelessness scale" contains twenty statements which are scored true or false. People who have a very pessimistic view of the future are likely to get a high score, indicating a high intensity of hopeless feelings, as you can see from the scale on the following page.

Not everyone who scores high on the hopelessness test will commit suicide; in fact, the overwhelming majority of the patients with a high score did not commit suicide. The scale is, however, an instrument to estimate suicidal risk. The more we learn about the exact relationship between hopelessness and ultimate suicide, the greater the optimism that suicide can be predicted and prevented.

THE HOPELESSNESS SCALE

Key	Item

Key		
True	2.	I might as well give up because I can't make things better for myself.
	4.	I can't imagine what my life would be like in 10 years.
	7.	My future seems dark to me.
	9.	I just don't get the breaks, and there's no reason to believe I will in the future.
	11.	All I can see ahead of me is unpleasantness rather than pleasantness.
	12.	I don't expect to get what I really want.
	14.	Things just won't work out the way I want them to.
	16.	I never get what I want so it's foolish to want anything.
	17.	It is very unlikely that I will get any real satisfaction in the future.
	18.	The future seems vague and uncertain to me.
	20.	There's no use in really trying to get something I want because I probably won't get it.

False 1. I look forward to the future with hope and enthusiasm.
3. When things are going badly, I am helped by knowing they can't stay that way forever.
5. I have enough time to accomplish the things I most want to do.
6. In the future, I expect to succeed in what concerns me most.
8. I expect to get more of the good things in life than the average person.
10. My past experiences have prepared me well for my future.
13. When I look ahead to the future, I expect I will be happier then than I am now.
15. I have great faith in the future.
19. I can look forward to more good times than bad times.

Source: M. Kovacs, A. T. Beck, and M. A. Weissman, "Hopelessness: An Indicator of Suicidal Risk," *Suicide*, vol. 5, no. 2 (Summer 1975), pp. 98–103.

SCHIZOPHRENIA

Twenty-five percent of all hospital beds in the United States are occupied by schizophrenics. Schizophrenia is a condition that is characterized by disturbances of thinking, mood, and behavior, and often by distortions of the person's ability to perceive reality correctly. Sometimes people suffering from this disorder form delusional ideas or experience hallucinations. In this state, occasionally a person may kill himself or herself in response to voices or in order to escape imagined persecution.

In a study of suicide among schizophrenic mental hospital patients, reported by Dr. Norman L. Farberow and others, it was found that contrary to what one might suppose, most of the patients studied did not commit suicide in a psychotic, delusional state. In fact, most of those who committed suicide were considered to have improved in terms of their illness. Almost all had "good reasons" for their suicides. Three types of suicidal patients were identified, and although these people differed from each other in their behavior and attitudes, they were found to have an important characteristic in common. They all saw their illness as a very stressful situation from which they were not able to escape. In contrast to those who committed suicide, the control group (hospitalized schizophrenics who did not commit suicide) were found to be people who seemed able to adjust to their illness and live with it.

As noted earlier, Dr. Eugene Paykel has shown that suicide attempts are preceded by a high concentration of stressful events. The occurrence of schizophrenia, as well, has been linked with stressful events.

CHAPTER

8

GROWING UP SUICIDAL

Recently, some adolescents were interviewed for a television news broadcast. They were intelligent, attractive young people who had one thing in common—they had all attempted suicide. Most of them commented that they found it difficult to talk to their parents. Some parents were too busy to listen, while others laughed at the idea of a young person wanting to die. One girl said that her father had dismissed her suicidal feelings as a "phase" that would pass. A very high percentage of suicidal teenagers think their families do not understand them. These feelings are common; many teenagers feel misunderstood, but certainly not all of them attempt suicide.

GROWING UP "DEAD"

Dr. Herbert Hendin has treated many college students who have made suicide attempts, and has found that for many, death has been a way of life. They have been emotionally dead all their lives, and suicide was giving reality to a state that already existed. Dr. Hendin notes that death, depression, and unhappiness seem to have been with them since childhood, and have been built into their relationships with their parents.

Many families are so full of anger and anxiety that the only way to survive is for both parents and children to bury their feelings within themselves. However, an acute awareness still remains that something is missing from their lives. For example, Jean was a talented, well-educated young woman who had been depressed for a long time because of the emptiness and loneliness of her life. She was unable to enjoy anything she did and took no pleasure in her very real artistic accomplishments.

She complained of having no feelings at all; she denied ever feeling anger or love or happiness. Jean had grown up in a family where there had been no love, trust, or other good feelings; she remembered only conflict. Both parents had been very rejecting and abusive toward her, and her mother, who had been psychotic, died when Jean was nine years old. Her mother had often impressed on her the necessity of squelching her feelings as a means of survival. Jean had a long history of self-destructive behavior, often slashing herself with a razor blade. One of the reasons she gave was that only at these times was she able to feel anything; pain was better than no feelings at all. On several occasions, Jean made serious suicide attempts, usually when she felt especially worthless and wanted to punish herself for something. Often, these attempts came after an encounter during which she had not expressed appropriate anger or annoyance at another person. She commented that she had something bad inside that she needed to kill. It turned out that the bad thing in her was the internalized image of her mother, whom she thought of as a demon or spirit in her head.

Although Jean's case is a very complicated and somewhat extreme example, it points up several themes that are repeated with variations in many instances of suicide. She had a background of emotional rejection by her parents and at age nine experienced the death of her mother. During her childhood, she experienced many other stressful situations within her family. She was unable to express anger or direct hostility toward others, so she turned it inward against herself, and at the same time, against her mother. Her self-image was very low, and she felt worthless and incompetent. She saw herself as helpless and not in control of her own life; since she could not allow herself to express her needs or feelings, she often put others in the position of telling her what to do. In this way, she perpetuated the helplessness that she had learned as a child. Because she saw no way of changing, her future looked bleak, and her outlook on life was hopeless. Jean is a sad example of a person who has grown up dead.

LOOKING AT
ADOLESCENT SUICIDE

Dr. Stuart M. Finch and Dr. Elva O. Poznanski of the University of Michigan Medical School have attempted to draw some conclusions about adolescent suicide by looking at the families and at the personalities of young people who have shown suicidal behavior. While many studies were found to show conflicting results, and other studies were based mainly on subjective impressions, they are nevertheless useful in adding to our knowledge about suicide.

Many adolescents do not show any recognizable signs of suicidal behavior in the three months preceding their suicide attempts. In many instances, the precipitating event seemed trivial on the surface. The suicide attempt appeared to be a sudden, impulsive reaction to a stressful situation, such as a quarrel with parents or the breaking up of a romance.

A large proportion of suicidal adolescents seemed to show long-standing patterns of impulsive behavior. Many drove beyond the speed limit, accepted dares, and were easily aroused to anger. Most were attempters, but some succeeded in killing themselves. A number were individuals who could not deal with their problems in socially acceptable ways. They usually denied having any problems, and many denied serious motives for their suicide attempts. Many had had suicidal ideas before. Often, there were obvious elements of revenge or spite directed against their families, or manipulative behavior—"emotional blackmail" with the purpose of arousing guilt.

Although some people think that all who commit suicide are mentally ill, only a small percentage of suicidal adolescents are psychotic. The reasons for suicide among psychotics are not always as obvious as in the case of impulsive teenagers, or of those who show clear signs of depression.

SUICIDAL PRESCHOOLERS

Death by suicide by preschoolers is rare. But suicidal behavior in young children is distressingly common. Some very young children who were asked about "accidents" admitted that these were suicide attempts. A suicidal group of preschoolers was compared with a group of behaviorally disordered preschoolers, matched by age, sex, race, parental marriage state, and socioeconomic status. The suicidal group showed much less pain and cried less after injury. They had greater loss of interest and more morbid ideas, depression, impulsivity, hyperactivity, and running-away behavior. More of the suicidal children were unwanted and either abused or neglected by their parents.

In another study, suicidal children had early experiences of separation and loss. Death of, or separation from, a parent or grandparent, death of a sibling or pet, and loss of personal possessions were noted in 80 percent of the suicidal group. Sixty-five percent witnessed violent fights between their parents and 60 percent were physically abused themselves.

Some suicidal children think that death is reversible and see suicide as a way to reunite with a parent lost through divorce or death. Some children try to punish themselves or escape from an intolerable home life. These children tend to see death as irreversible.

Young suicide attempters use violent methods such as hanging, running into traffic, drowning, stabbing, and poisoning. Although preschool suicide is rare, families and others should take notice and take action if a child talks about wanting to die.

SUICIDE AND ADOLESCENT AGGRESSION

Although adolescence is normally a time of increased conflict, suicidal teenagers seem to have more difficulties than others in resolving their problems. Many have had a lifelong history of problems, with more than the normal increase during adolescence. Additional stress, such as some disturbance in a meaningful personal relationship, may then result in a suicide attempt.

The relationship between suicide and aggression has been discussed earlier. According to some writers, most people are born with a "reasonable amount" of innate aggression. Individuals who have been taught to handle their aggression well are able to assert themselves in healthy ways.

Some people may be born with an unusually high aggressive drive. Others may be subject to an increased amount of frustration from their families or society, which may lead to hostile aggression. During adolescence, when there is a normal increase in aggression, such individuals may experience special problems. The aggression may be turned inward or outward. Often, these people may express feelings of hostility toward themselves and others at the same time. It is not difficult to understand the close relationship between suicide and homicide, and the not uncommon newspaper accounts of homicide followed by suicide.

SOME SPECIAL PROBLEMS

Adolescents who are prone to suicide may have more than the usual problems in attempting to find their identity and in attaining independence. Many are highly ambivalent about growing up, and remain abnormally dependent, because they equate independence with the loss of parental love. Overly dependent people are more susceptible to loss, and may react with suicidal behavior in an attempt to gratify their wishes to be cared for.

School problems have been associated with suicide in adolescents as well as children. In one study, an estimated one-third of the adolescent suicide attempters were found to have dropped out of school because of behavior problems rather than academic difficulties. The school problems in these cases were the result of long-standing emotional difficulties which were also the fore-runners of suicide.

A low percentage of suicides are of the "contagious" variety. These are most frequent in small groups of disturbed adolescents, who may be so fearful of losing status because of nonconformity that they prefer to lose their lives instead. This can happen in almost any neighborhood or environment. The recent cluster suicides that have made newspaper headlines have alerted readers to the whole problem of adolescent suicide.

SEXUAL PROBLEMS

In the *Journal of the Canadian Psychiatric Association*, a study was reported in which one-third of the suicidal adolescent females interviewed had been seduced by their fathers. This experience is so painful and produces such strong guilt feelings that it is not surprising that sexual conflicts are among the problems associated with suicidal behavior. Incestuous preoccupations in girls who attempt suicide are not uncommon, according to some.

In some instances, adolescent boys have strangled themselves, possibly by accident, while engaging in activities that were sexually stimulating. Many were found with ropes around their limbs as well as their necks, and some have been dressed in women's clothing. These adolescents presumably derived sexual pleasure from the acting out of their fantasies. It is difficult to determine how many boys actually wanted to commit suicide.

HOSTILE FAMILIES

Many people have wondered what kind of family environment fosters the development of suicidal children. Some experts think that there has been an increase in hidden hostility against children in many families. Dr. Herbert Hendin, as noted earlier, has commented on the negative feelings and covert ambivalence present in the families of suicidal students whom he treated.

Often, parental attitudes appear to be very ambivalent toward the suicidal adolescent. About half of the parents in one study were found to have conveyed to their children the feeling that they were unwanted and too much trouble. Some researchers have used the term "expendable child" in this connection. Sometimes the suicide attempt seemed to have been triggered directly by a hostile or rejecting comment from a parent. Unbelievable as it may seem, there have been many instances in which the family of a suicidal youngster does not take the proper precautions and "forgets" to remove guns or drugs from the house. In these cases, suicide may be the result of carrying out the family's unconscious hostile wishes.

In other families, the emotional deprivation is not hidden. Many suicidal adolescents come from homes that are characterized by disorganization, parental disharmony, cruelty, and abandonment. In many instances, a successful suicide has two ingredients—a hostile, rejecting family, and an adolescent who cannot retaliate in any way except to commit suicide.

Some suicidal adolescents grow up in families who push their children too hard to perform at school, in sports, and socially. Often, these parents are attempting to live out their own fantasies through their children. The parents try to impose their own standards and goals without listening to what their children have to say. While both children and adolescents need and want some guidance, they need to develop independence at the same time. They also need supportive parents who are not constantly demanding perfection. Some adolescents who feel that they cannot measure up to their parents' expectations may become depressed and suicidal.

PARENTAL LOSS

Much has been written about parental loss as a factor in depression and in suicide. Studies have shown that from 44 to 66 percent of adolescents who attempted or completed suicide come from broken homes. But it is extremely difficult to assess the effects of parental loss and broken homes, because there are so many other variables at work. Parental loss may be more significant if it occurs at an early age; repeated separations may be more traumatic than a single loss. In addition, the outcome depends on the ability of the remaining parent or other family members to meet the child's needs and to deal with his or her problems.

Experts note that today's young adults face more choices, have greater freedom and fewer limits than ever before. Some people from loving homes kill themselves. Suicide may be viewed as an attempt to escape from, or as a way of expressing anger about, such "modern ills" as frequent moves to new neighborhoods and schools, family crises such as divorce, death, or peer pressure, pressure to achieve, a failed romance, or any other of life's stresses.

Much needs to be investigated about the complex subject of causes of suicide. This discussion has only touched on some of the important points that may play a part in growing up dead. Each case is individual.

CHAPTER

9

WHO COMMITS SUICIDE? CONFLICTING STATISTICS

Few people argue that suicide is one of the ten leading causes of death in the United States and is the second or third most frequent cause of death among teenagers and young adults. Few argue that suicide rates vary in different countries and cultures. Few argue that suicide afflicts all segments of society—the young and the old, the poor and rich, males and females, and people of all races and ethnic groups. But statistics on suicides are conflicting. They attempt to present a scientific evaluation of a highly emotional and individual act, and they are far from accurate, but statistics do help to assess the risk to any person in a crisis by serving as a general guide in determining who is most vulnerable. Statistics also help in research on the causes of suicide.

SUICIDE AND GENDER

A statistic that once appeared to be stable was that concerning gender. For many years, statistics showed that more men than women committed suicide. The ratio was three men to one woman. Just the reverse was true for attempted suicides—according to statistics, women led men in attempts by a ratio of three to one. But over the past twenty years, the incidence of suicide among women has risen more than for men, especially among people from forty-five to forty-nine years of age. While the rate of increase has almost tripled for both sexes in the teens and twenties, it has dropped by almost 50 percent in the old-age group. Old age used to be the peak period for both sexes.

Many explanations are offered for the changing trend. Among them is the theory that women are using more lethal means in their suicide attempts than in previous years. Historically, most men have chosen hanging, shooting, and jumping from heights. The majority of women have used drugs and they may still be more apt to use them than more violent means. But today, women may be more knowledgeable about how much of a drug is lethal in addition to having a greater willingness to use more violent means such as shooting or hanging.

Present-day mobility and lack of roots, weakened family structures, and increased pressures to succeed have all been suggested as playing a part in the trend toward higher suicide rates among females. An increasing number of women engaging in occupations formerly dominated by men may be subjecting themselves to increased stress. This has been considered as a possible cause for the increased suicide rate, but no one can be sure of this. It might well be true that housewives who committed suicide were, and still are, reported as having died from natural causes in an effort to prevent the stigma associated with suicide.

Two things are certain: first, no one really knows how many men and women commit suicide; and second, in both sexes, most suicides can be prevented.

SUICIDE AND RELIGION

Statistics have often indicated that more Protestants committed suicide than Catholics or Jews, but some authorities believe that religion is no longer a major factor in assessing suicide risk, especially in the United States. It does seem to hold true that in some countries where suicide is considered a mortal sin by large numbers of people, such as in Ireland and Egypt, rates appear to be low. Experts who have closely studied this aspect of statistics feel that time, place, and social circumstances play an important part, no matter what a person's religion.

SUICIDE AND GEOGRAPHY

Consider the case of West Berlin. Here, the suicide rate is believed to be the highest in the world, and it has been twice that of West Germany. Might this be due to alienation and classed as the type of suicide that Durkheim described as anomie? West Berlin is alienated geographically, socially, politically, and culturally. No one knows if the suicide rates for this city are completely accurate, but they do give evidence of an unusual situation.

Geography may influence people who live in isolated areas, in areas where the days are short and the nights are long, and/or where climate is especially rainy or cloudy. Various kinds of weather have been accused of increasing the number of suicides, but statistics vary so greatly that it is impossible to draw any useful conclusions.

WHITES AND BLACKS

Suicides have generally been greater among whites than among blacks. But black suicide is on the rise, especially among the young. The suicide rate for black males in their early twenties has shown an alarming increase, and much suicide among young black people is thought to be caused by feelings of failure and hopelessness.

Consider the case of Ray. He was the pride of his family and was the only one of them to enter college. The family called him their ticket to a better future, and each member of the family worked in some way to contribute to Ray's education. When things did not go well at school, Ray told his roommate that he felt as if he were letting his family down. Fear of failure had always made Ray unhappy at college, and now that fear seemed to be based on fact. Ray knew he could not go to summer school to make up the course he was failing because he needed the money from summer work to supplement his scholarship. One week he found himself in a very threatening situation. He could not keep up with the pace of the work, partly because of his poor educational background and partly because of his depression. So Ray bought a term paper from another student who had used it several years before. Ray worried about the possibility that the instructor might recognize the paper, but he was too depressed to concentrate on writing one for himself. He felt he had to take the risk.

What seemed almost impossible happened. The paper was recognized. Ray was in danger of losing his scholarship. He was in danger of not graduating. The day he appeared before the student council for a hearing about his actions, Ray told his roommate he would be better off dead. The roommate tried to cheer him by telling him that he was better off than most people and that he would feel better in a few weeks. But before the weeks passed, Ray had hanged himself in his room.

Help could have come from his roommate if he had recognized the clues that Ray was giving. Help might have come from a call to a suicide-prevention center, but Ray had not heard about such places. He became one more statistic in the growing number of blacks who are taking their own lives.

Environments in which there is crime and violence, drug abuse, and/or a missing father figure seem to make a person especially vulnerable, whether black or white. Among both groups, unrealized hopes and promises seem to play a major part in producing suicidal feelings. Not everyone agrees, but some people believe that blacks are more vulnerable because they are more apt to be put in a situation where there is nothing to strive for and where the future seems hopeless.

PROBLEMS OF INTERPRETATION

One of the difficulties with suicide statistics is the obvious problem of not being able to communicate with the person who has taken his or her life. Even when notes are left, the content may not offer much information about the seriousness of the attempt, leaving some question as to whether or not the death was accidental. If the cause of death is not clear, many people choose to claim death by natural causes in order to avoid stigma for the family of the victim. The following cases illustrate how interpretations vary.

Situation ■ A man, age thirty-five, was warned that continued drinking would surely kill him since his liver and digestive system were already damaged. He continued to drink heavily, and died within a year of the warnings. The cause of death was listed as natural.

Situation ■ A woman, age twenty-five, was depressed over her career situation. She threatened suicide several times. While driving her car, she crashed into a tree. No skid marks were observed, indicating she had not tried to brake the car. The cause of death was listed as accidental.

Situation ■ A man, age twenty, formerly had been a patient in a mental hospital. He had been diagnosed as schizophrenic but had shown definite improvement in recent weeks. He jumped or fell from a window on the tenth floor of his apartment building. The cause of death was never determined.

Situation ■ A woman, age nineteen, wanted to manipulate her father into buying a car. She left a note saying that she had taken an overdose of barbiturates and was sorry that her father could not understand her inability to live without a car. She arranged to be in a hallway where her father always entered the house on returning from work at 5 P.M. The woman took the pills just before 5 P.M. but her father was delayed that day and no one came home until 8 P.M. The cause of death was listed as suicide.

HIDDEN SUICIDES

In addition to the confusing picture that would result from any statistics compiled from the above situations, there are numerous kinds of hidden suicides. People who take great risks, who overeat, drink too much, experiment with drugs, smoke too much, and indulge in other forms of self-destructive behavior might be counted as unconscious or slow suicides. There are people who precipitate their murder as a form of suicide.

STATISTICS AND PEOPLE

Large numbers of charts exist that reveal the statistics on those who committed suicide in different years and different places. These charts contain such classifications as locality (urban or rural); sex; race; time of the year, month, and day; and so forth. Some of these charts help suicidologists to observe trends and are useful in research. But a look at the problems of families and the individual people in them may be more meaningful than all the statistics in the world.

CHAPTER

10

PREVENTION: WHAT TO DO AND WHAT NOT TO DO

Youth suicide is a tragic waste of life. Undecided, wavering, almost always young people who commit suicide ask to be saved from themselves right up to the time of death. Ask, but are not heard.

Most suicides can be prevented. You can help by knowing the danger signs, knowing what are some of the things you can say to a suicidal person, and what to do and what not to do.

Suppose Jill confides in a friend that she is tired of living. The conversation might go like this:

"I feel rotten. I might as well be dead," Jill says.

One of her friends may offer the advice, "Get it together, Jill. You can hack it."

Another friend might tell her to think how lucky she is. Their friend Mary has cancer, but she is not depressed. "And Mary may not live more than a year."

"She's lucky," is the response from Jill. That makes her friends uncomfortable, but they decide to forget it. "Jill isn't the suicidal type," they tell each other.

One close friend, in whom Jill has confided her

actual suicide *plans* wants to keep her promise not to tell on Jill because, "Jill would never forgive me if I broke my promise." She tells herself that Jill will feel better tomorrow. Of course, that could happen.

But what if, when tomorrow comes Jill drives her car around a curve at high speed and crashes into a large tree, killing herself. The accident upsets the whole class, but the friends who suspected her death was not an accident are shocked, almost beyond themselves. They know they did not listen to Jill's hints—her cry for help. The friend in whom she confided her "secret" feels two kinds of grief: the loss of someone close to her, and the guilt and sorrow of knowing she could have told the secret to someone who might have very easily persuaded Jill that there were other alternatives.

One of the first steps in prevention is a change in attitude about suicide. We can recognize the clues and not back away. Most people who are thinking of suicide reveal their thoughts directly or indirectly, giving friends or family a chance to direct them to a source of help via phone contact with a crisis-center counselor, a member of clergy, or school counselor. There are many people offering help. You can be among them if you direct someone to professional assistance.

CLUES TO SUICIDE

Preoccupation with Thoughts of Death ■ Verbal clues can be very faint. Someone can ask about the hereafter in connection with a third person, or talk about another person's suicidal thoughts or plans. Ideas about heaven or hell are hints about thoughts of death, even when talked about "objectively."

Statements of Worthlessness ■ Most suicidal young people feel mild depression and suffer poor self-esteem. Usually, an event triggers loss of faith in oneself; a time of danger. These can range from a bad grade on an exam, losing an after-school job, an argument with a friend of either sex, inability to pay a debt, the loss or illness of a parent, or a change in life-style.

A Settling of Affairs ■ Concern about life insurance, wills, and other documents can indicate suicidal plans. While many adults normally are concerned about these things, those with suicidal intent may show more obvious concern as an unconscious way of asking for help.

Giving Away Prized Possessions ■ People of all ages may be signaling their suicidal mentality when they give away, for no apparent reason, prized possessions such as cameras and jewelry, or any variety of material things. Sometimes they remark that these things will not be "needed" anymore. Some people act as if they are going on a trip. This "generosity" should set off an alarm.

Suicide Threats ■ The false belief that, "people who say they are going to kill themselves never do," has long been disproved. "I really didn't think he (she) would do it," is a remark that is often made by people who ignored suicide threats. Every suicide threat should be taken very seriously.

Depression ■ Common symptoms of depression are crying, sleeplessness, loss of appetite, isolation, and hopelessness. The relationship of depression and suicide has been discussed earlier. When a person is more withdrawn, uncommunicative, and isolated from others than usual, he or she may be sending out a warning signal. Question that person if necessary.

Possession of Suicidal Plans ■ Question a person who appears to you to be suicidal to determine if any detailed suicide plans have been made, the details of the plan, and whether or not any beginning action has been taken. Any hints of such plans call for IMMEDIATE HELP from a crisis center.

Accidental Poisoning and Self-Destructive Behavior ■ What appears to be accidental self-poisoning, such as pills combined with alcohol, is likely to be an attempt at self-destruction, especially in the adolescent years. If you have a friend who has had several episodes of self-poisoning, take this as a strong clue to suicidal intent. The intent may be unconscious, and therefore unclear. This friend needs counseling.

A suicidal gesture by adolescents may come before the act of self-destruction as often as three times when "accidental" poisoning occurs. In drug overdoses, drugs most commonly used are aspirin, Tylenol, Dalmane and Valium in combination with each other or with alcohol. Some of these combinations cause permanent brain damage instead of death.

A Sudden Apparent Peace of Mind ■ Knowing the above clues is not always enough, for the clues may be missed even by professionals who are trained to understand people's feelings. In one case, a woman who was being treated by a psychiatrist for severe depression appeared to be much better. The psychiatrist was pleased with the woman's apparent peace of mind. But after the patient left the doctor's office, she went home and swallowed all the sleeping pills in the bottle next to her bed. After the suicide, the psychiatrist and others who had known the woman put together some of the clues to the puzzle and wondered why they had not recognized the warning signals. They realized the woman had resolved her conflict about whether to live or to die, but that she did not express this in words. The clue: her tranquility or peace of mind.

Knowing whether or not any of the above are serious warning signals can be difficult even for a professional, but it is better to make an error on the side of suspicion. All of the clues or signals here, and others, give hints to those who really listen. Use your intuition, or common sense. Sometimes friends can recognize a suicidal intention by a change in manner. Sudden passivity, a giving up, make them "just know"' something is terribly wrong. And something is. Any sign that someone is considering suicide is an alarm, a call to action. Respond.

WHAT TO DO

Believe It ■ When someone talks of suicide, he or she should be taken very seriously. Accept what is said, and try to focus on the problem. If you have a good relationship with the person, you might want to be frank with your concern. Ask the person if he or she is thinking about giving up on life, or ending it all.

Listen ■ A person who is feeling suicidal is in a state of emotional crisis and needs someone who will listen. By reflecting back the person's feelings you can help that person to feel that someone has heard his or her pain. Acknowledge the person's feelings of helplessness. You can say, "I can see how you feel." By listening, you are being supportive; you are showing you care. Ask questions, talk calmly, listen carefully and sympathize.

Get Help ■ No matter what you yourself conclude about the intensity of the crisis, you must get help. Call a suicide-prevention center, crisis-intervention clinic, mental-health clinic, physician, hospital emergency room, or religious adviser. A reliable family member can be told, one who will get more help. If you believe the person is in danger of taking action at once, do not leave him or her. Talk about the problem and lead the person to one of the above places. If you feel that the situation is immediately life-threatening, call the police.

Remove Weapons of Choice ■ If you learn about actual, specific plans that have been made toward suicide, you can be almost sure that the risk is greater than if they are vague. Stay with the person, if possible, and get help. Remove any self-destructive weapons the person talked about.

WHAT NOT TO DO

Do Not Give Advice ■ Other than seeking help for the person, you should not try to offer such advice as, "Everything will be all right," or, "Snap out of it." Do not be judgmental.

Do not swear secrecy.

Do not debate whether suicide is right or wrong.

Do not increase guilt.

"Think how your parents, friends, etc., would feel" will not help a person who feels anger or helplessness. Avoid such remarks as, "Be grateful for what you have. You are much better off than most people." This can make the person feel more worthless than if you had said nothing. The last thing a suicidal person needs is a lecture. If he or she could feel empathy for other people and pull out of the depression or hopeless state, suicide would not be part of the picture.

Do Not Delay Dealing with the Situation ■ Do not leave the person alone if you think the risk is immediate. Call a suicide-prevention center. If you are not near a telephone, invent an excuse that will make the person go with you to a place where there is a phone.

Never Tell a Person that He or She Is Just Fooling ■ Not being believed would increase despair and might serve as a challenge that could start self-destructive actions. Sometimes it is possible to deter a suicidal person by removing the weapons of choice. One might think that removing knives or guns would only change the mode of suicide, but it has been shown that many people plan to do away with themselves by a certain method and do not resort to others if that method is unavailable.

A suicide is often a matter that involves two people. Those who work at suicide-prevention centers have found that there are cases where a "significant other" is helping the suicidal person to carry out his or her wishes. This may be unconscious, or it may be blatant. In at least one case, the "significant other" has been known to have hidden a gun under the mattress of the suicidal person. Therapists are able to discover and deal with the interplay between the suicidal person and the other person involved, but this takes training. But removing obvious things that might be used in suicide plans is something that any caring person can do on finding that someone in the family has given clues to their suicide.

SUICIDE PREVENTION
IN THE CLASSROOM

A growing number of communities are accepting the idea of teaching suicide prevention in the schools as part of their health education programs. Individuals who are concerned about the possible increase in youth suicide or simply want to save even one life, can suggest such programs to their counselors, health education teachers, and principals. They can ask their parents to bring up the subject at Parent-Teacher-Association or other organization meetings.

Schools where one (or more) students have committed suicide can galvanize the attention given to the tragedy and start a teaching program. After four young people took their lives within an eighteen-month period, the Cherry Creek school district in Denver, Colorado, began a program of class discussions with students, and held parent workshops and volunteer training seminars for teachers, counselors, and nurses who work in the seven secondary schools of that district.

Students, in their seventh- and eighth-grade suicide-prevention discussions, learn the danger of keeping threats as secrets and are encouraged to tell a counselor of threats they hear. They learn to openly discuss their feelings about depression and suicide. These students know not to panic if they feel depressed or overwhelmed and how to use community resources to help themselves and others. They learn alternatives to suicide. There are ways of dealing with a painful life. All these skills strengthen them. Having those insights, and better ways to cope with life's stresses, brings these students closer together.

A parent who attended a workshop learned the way to cope with her child's statements about suicide and how to help. She asked questions about her twelve-year-old, a boy who had threatened suicide. It turned out he even had a plan to hang himself in the garage. Immediate action led to hospitalization where medication and counseling lessened his depression in a period of three weeks. A life was saved.

Teachers learn to spot suicidal themes in writing assignments and artwork and to take action to help troubled young people.

There have been no suicides in Cherry Creek since the program began about five years ago. Other school systems are working with similar programs. All such programs broaden the students' vision of life and increase the values we call "human" — hope, imagination, and care for others.

NATIONAL COMMITTEE
FOR THE PREVENTION
OF YOUTH SUICIDE

Created in 1984 under the direction of New York State Lieutenant Governor Alfred B. DelBello, this group is aimed at organizing state-by-state efforts to educate the public about the national tragedy of youth suicide. They pressure, or lobby, Congress for the establishment of a National Commission on Teenage Suicide Prevention. This Commission could study the causes of young suicide in the United States and help guide state and local governments in the development of programs to aid prevention of youth suicides.

Many experts in the field of suicide prevention want to establish a national data base, and to research and analyze the causes of teenage suicide. A National Commission could form the policy directions for the federal government, and provide direction to state and local governments and school systems in the development of preventive programs. Working together, communities, schools, and parents can build programs based upon positives, including the universal will to life.

SUICIDE-PREVENTION
CENTERS

What happens at a suicide-prevention center when a person calls for help depends partly on the individual case. But in each case, the person who answers the phone concentrates on getting the caller over the crisis. As with all hotlines, there is the policy of anonymity unless the caller wishes to be identified. In the case of a suicidal crisis, the worker tries to get information about the location of the person if that person seems on the verge of taking action. Then, help can be sent. But if this information is held back, the suicide-prevention worker can ask questions and talk with the caller only in such a way that he or she calms the individual by providing emotional support, and helps the person past the immediate state of tunnel vision. Alternatives to suicide are then possible.

No one knows how many lives are saved by any suicide-prevention center. Many people who call may not be very serious about taking their lives. But in the great majority of cases, they want and need help, and this is what is available. In the case of the Los Angeles Suicide Prevention Center, Co-Director Norman Farberow reports that follow-up studies indicate that the center is of considerable help. When questioned a short time after their calls, 87 percent of the people said that they had been helped. When questioned a long time after their calls, 80 percent maintained they had been helped. Twenty-eight percent said that the center had saved their lives and another 34 percent said that it might have saved their lives.

The number of calls to suicide-prevention centers continues to mount each year, and the number of centers is growing. Some areas are developing programs that reach out far from the counseling center. For example in Bangor, Maine, Dial Help encompasses an area of 12,000 square miles with the main clinic in Bangor and satellite clinics in several of the larger communities. When a person who is feeling suicidal calls Dial Help, the volunteer answering the phone consults a professional who is on call to determine whether or not the situation is serious enough to bring in the crisis worker in the area. If it is, the volunteer calls the team member in the rural area and provides that worker with the necessary information. In some cases, face-to-face intervention is attempted by the team member and another volunteer who assists with such crises. The professional on call is kept abreast of the situation by following the communication between the volunteer in the community and Dial Help.

As with other volunteers, the community crisis workers are carefully screened, and they are trained in suicide intervention and in ways to help a person after the crisis is over. They are supervised on a regular basis just as telephone crisis counselors are, but community workers are also trained in face-to-face intervention. This technique has proved very helpful in areas where geography makes it impossible for professionals to get to places where people are attempting to take their own lives.

THE AMERICAN ASSOCIATION OF SUICIDOLOGY

In order to further the goal of suicide prevention, the American Association of Suicidology was founded in the United States in 1968 by Professor Edwin Shneidman. He was chief of the Center for Studies of Suicide Prevention at the National Institute of Mental Health at that time. Today, this association has several hundred Suicide and Crisis Intervention Centers in its membership along with individuals who are interested in similar goals. A list of these centers appears at the back of this book.

One of the important functions of the American Association of Suicidology is the development of programs and activities that can alleviate the anguish and cost of suicide. The association enlists the support of people in many professions and coordinates the efforts of individual communities in the area of suicide prevention. In addition to sponsoring conferences and publications for the public and researchers, it sponsors awareness programs. Throughout the year, media announcements help to acquaint people with the suicide-prevention and crisis-intervention services available to them in their local communities. Another major goal of the association is to educate people to better recognize and respond to suicidal behavior.

Although the enigma of suicide remains unsolved, you may now know what to say to a suicidal person and know how to act to help save a life.

SUICIDE PREVENTION/ CRISIS INTERVENTION AGENCIES IN THE UNITED STATES AND CANADA

ALASKA

ANCHORAGE

*#Suicide Prevention and Crisis
  Center
2611 Fairbanks St.
Anchorage, AK 99503
Crisis Phone 1: (907) 276-1600
Business Phone: (907) 272-2496

FAIRBANKS

*#Fairbanks Crisis Clinic
  Foundation
P.O. Box 832
Fairbanks, AK 99707
Crisis Phone 1: (907) 452-4403
Business Phone: (907) 479-0166

JUNEAU

Juneau Mental Health Clinic
210 Admiral Way
Juneau, AK 99801
Crisis Phone 1: (907) 586-5280
Crisis Phone 2: (907) 789-4889
Business Phone: (907) 586-5280

ALABAMA

AUBURN

Crisis Center of E. Alabama,
  Inc.
P.O. Box 1949
Auburn, AL 36830
Crisis Phone 1: (205) 821-8600
Business Phone: (205) 821-8600

BIRMINGHAM

*#Crisis Center of Jefferson
County
3600 8th Ave. S.
Birmingham, AL 35222
Crisis Center: (205) 323-7777
Business Phone: (205) 323-7782

DECATUR

Crisis Call Center
North Central Alabama MH
Center
P.O. Box 637
Decatur, AL 35601
Crisis Phone 1: (205) 355–6091
Business Phone: (205) 355-6091

HUNTSVILLE

Huntsville Helpline
P.O. Box 92
Huntsville, AL 35804
Crisis Phone 1: (205) 539-3424
Business Phone: (205) 534-1779

MOBILE

* Contact Mobile
3224 Executive Park Circle
Mobile, AL 36606
Crisis Phone 1: (205) 342-3333
Business Phone: (205) 473-5330

MONTGOMERY

Help a Crisis
101 Coliseium Boulevard
Montgomery, AL 36109
Crisis Phone 1: (205) 279-7837
Business Phone: (205) 279-7830

TUSCALOOSA

Indian Rivers Mental Health
Center
Tuscaloosa Crisis Line
P.O. Box 2190
Tuscaloosa, AL 35403
Crisis Phone 1: (205) 345-1600
Business Phone: (205) 345-1600

ARKANSAS

HOT SPRINGS

Contact Hot Springs
705 Malvern Ave.
Hot Springs, AR 71901
Crisis Phone 1: (501) 623-2515
Business Phone: (501) 623-4048

LITTLE ROCK

Crisis Center of Arkansas, Inc.
1616 W. 14th St.
Little Rock, AR 72202
Crisis Phone 1: (501) 375-5151
Business Phone: (501) 664-8834

PINE BLUFF

Contact Pine Bluff
P.O. Box 8734
Pine Bluff, AR 71601
Crisis Phone 1: (501) 536-4226
Business Phone: (501) 536-4228

ARIZONA

PHOENIX

Phoenix Crisis Intervention
Program
1250 S. 7th Ave.
Phoenix, AZ 85007
Crisis Phone 1: (602) 258-8011
Business Phone: (602) 258-8011

Tucson

Tucson Help on Call
Information and Referral
  Service
2555 E. First St., Suite #107
Tucson, AZ 85716
Crisis Phone 1: (602) 323-9373
Business Phone: (602) 323-1303

CALIFORNIA

Anaheim

* Hotline Help Center
P.O. Box 999
Anaheim, CA 92805
Crisis Phone 1: (714) 778-1000
Business Phone: (714) 778-1000

Berkeley

* Suicide Prevention/Crisis
  Intervention of
  Alameda County
P.O. Box 9102
Berkeley, CA 94709
Crisis Phone 1: (415) 849-2212
Crisis Phone 2: (415) 889-1333
Crisis Phone 3: (415) 794-5211
Crisis Phone 4: (415) 449-5566
Business Phone: (415) 848-1515

San Mateo County

*#Suicide Prev./CC of San
  Mateo County
1811 Trousdale Dr.
Burlingame, CA 94010
Crisis Phone 1: (415) 877-5600
Crisis Phone 2: (415) 367-8000
Crisis Phone 3: (415) 726-5228
Business Phone: (415) 877-5604

Santa Cruz County

* SPS of Santa Cruz County
P.O. Box 734
Capitola, CA 95010
Crisis Phone 1: (408) 426-2342
Crisis Phone 2: (408) 688-6581
Business Phone: (408) 426-2342

Davis

* Suicide Prevention of Yolo
  County
P.O. Box 622
Davis, CA 95617
Crisis Phone 1: (916) 756-5000
Crisis Phone 2: (916) 666-7778
Crisis Phone 3: (916) 372-6565
Business Phone: (916) 756-7542

El Cajon

Crisis House/Crisis Interven-
  tion Center
144 S. Orange
El Cajon, CA 92020
Crisis Phone 1: (714) 444-1194
Business Phone: (714) 444-6506

Fresno

* Help in Emotional Trouble
P.O. Box 4282
Fresno, CA 93744
Crisis Phone 1: (209) 485-1432
Business Phone: (209) 486-4703

Ft. Bragg

Crisis Line Care Project
461 N. Franklin St.
P.O. Box 764
Ft. Bragg, CA 95437
Crisis Phone 1: (707) 964-4357
Business Phone: (707) 964-4055

Los Angeles

*#Los Angeles SPC
1041 S. Menlo
Los Angeles, CA 90006
Crisis Phone 1: (213) 381-5111
Business Phone: (213) 386-5111

Napa

* North Bay Suicide Prevention,
Inc.
P.O. Box 2444
Napa, CA 94558
Fairfield: (707) 422-2555
Napa: (707) 255-2555
Vallejo: (707) 643-2555
Business Phone: (707) 257-3470

Pacific Grove

* Suicide Prevention Center/
Monterey County
P.O. Box 52078
Pacific Grove, CA 93950-7078
Crisis Phone 1: (408) 649-8008
Salinas: (408) 424-1485
Business Phone: (408) 375-6966

Pasadena

Contact Pasadena
73 N. Hill Ave.
Pasadena, CA 91106
Crisis Phone 1: (818) 449-4500
Business Phone: (818) 449-4502

Pleasanton

✦ The Center
Counseling, Education, Crisis
Service
4361 Railroad Ave.; Suite B
Pleasanton, CA 94566
Crisis Phone 1: (415) 828-HELP
Business Phone: (415) 462-5544

Redding

* Help, Inc.
P.O. Box 2498
Redding, CA 96099
Crisis Phone 1: (916) 246-2711
Business Phone: (916) 225-5255

Riverside

Riverside Crisis & Outpatient
Service
9707 Magnolia St.
Riverside, CA 92503
Crisis Phone 1: (714) 351-7853
Business Phone: (714) 351-7861

Sacramento

* Suicide Prevention Service of
Sacramento
P.O. Box 449
Sacramento, CA 95802
Crisis Phone 1: (916) 441-1135
Business Phone: (916) 441-1138

San Anselmo

Marin Suicide Prevention
Center
P.O. Box 792
San Anselmo, CA 94960
Crisis Phone 1: (415) 454-4524
Business Phone: (415) 454-4566

San Bernadino

* Suicide & Crisis Intervention
Service
1669 N. "E" St.
San Bernadino, CA 92405
Crisis Phone 1: (714) 886-4889
Business Phone: (714) 886-6730

San Diego

*#The Crisis Team
P.O. Box 85524
San Diego, CA 92138
Crisis Phone 1: (619) 236-3339
Crisis Phone 2: (800) 351-0757
Business Phone: (619) 236-4576

San Francisco

* San Francisco Suicide Prevention
3940 Geary Blvd.
San Francisco, CA 94118
Crisis Phone 1: (415) 221-1423
Crisis Phone 2: (415) 221-1424
Crisis Phone 3: (415) 221-1428
Business Phone: (415) 752-4866

San Jose

* Santa Clara Suicide & Crisis Service
2220 Moorpark
San Jose, CA 95128
Crisis Phone 1: (408) 279-3312
Business Phone: (408) 279-6250

San Luis Obispo

San Luis Obispo County Hotline, Inc.
P.O. Box 654
San Luis Obispo, CA 93406
Crisis Phone 1: (805) 544-6162
Business Phone: (805) 544-6164

Santa Barbara

* Call-Line
P.O. Box 14567
Santa Barbara, CA 93107
Crisis Phone 1: (805) 569-2255
Business Phone: (805) 961-4114

Sonoma

Family Center Crisis Intervention Program
Sonoma Valley Family Center
Crisis Intervention Program
P.O. Box 128
Sonoma, CA 95476
Crisis Phone 1: (707) 938-HELP
Business Phone: (707) 996-7877

St. Helena

* Crisis-Help of Napa Valley, Inc.
1360 Adams St.
St. Helena, CA 94574
Crisis Phone 1: (707) 963-2555
Crisis Phone 2: (707) 944-2212
Business Phone: (707) 942-4319

Ventura

Crisis Evaluation Unit
Ventura County Mental Health Dept.
300 Hillmont Ave.
Ventura, CA 93003
Crisis Phone 1: (805) 652-6727
Business Phone: (805) 652-6727

Walnut Creek

* Contra Costa Crisis/Suicide Intervention
P.O. Box 4852
Walnut Creek, CA 94596
Crisis Phone 1: (415) 939-3232
Business Phone: (415) 939-1916

Yuba City

Sutter-Yuba MH Crisis Clinic
1965 Live Oak Blvd.
Yuba City, CA 95991
Crisis Phone 1: (916) 673-8255
Business Phone: (916) 674-8500

COLORADO

BOULDER

Emergency Psych. Services
1333 Iris Ave.
Boulder, CO 80302
Crisis Phone 1: (303) 447-1665
Business Phone: (303) 443-8500

COLORADO SPRINGS

Terros
P.O. Box 2642
Colorado Springs, CO 80901
Crisis Phone 1: (303) 471-4127
Business Phone: (303) 471-4128

DENVER

* Suicide and Crisis Control
2459 South Ash
Denver, CO 80222
Crisis Phone 1: (303) 757-0988
Crisis Phone 2: (303) 789-3073
Business Phone: (303) 756-8485

FT. COLLINS

* Crisis/Information Helpline of
Larimer County
700 W. Mountain Ave.
Ft. Collins, CO 80521-2506
Crisis Phone 1: (303) 493-3888
Business Phone: (303) 493-3896

GRAND JUNCTION

Grand Junction Helpline
P.O. Box 3302
Grand Junction, CO 81502
Crisis Phone 1: (303) 242-HELP
Business Phone: (303) 245-3270

PUEBLO

*#Pueblo Suicide Prevention,
Inc.
229 Colorado Ave.
Pueblo, CO 81004
Crisis Phone 1: (303) 544-1133
Business Phone: (303) 545-2477

CONNECTICUT

GREENWICH

* Hotline of Greenwich, Inc.
189 Mason St.
Greenwich, CT 06830
Crisis Phone 1: (203) 661-HELP
Business Phone: (203) 661-4378

NORWALK

Info Line of Southwestern
Connecticut
7 Academy St.
Norwalk, CT 06850
Bridgeport: (203) 333-7555

Norwalk: (203) 853-2525

Stamford: (203) 324-1010

Business Phone: (203) 333-7555

WESTPORT

Open Line, Ltd.
245 Post Road East
Westport, CT 06880
Crisis Phone 1: (203) 226-3546
Business Phone: (203) 226-3546

DELAWARE

GEORGETOWN

Georgetown Helpline
Sussex County Community
   MHC
Georgetown, DE 19947
Crisis Phone 1: (302) 856-6626
Business Phone: (302) 856-2151

NEW CASTLE

Psychiatric Emergency
   Services
S. New Castle County
   Community MH
14 Central Avenue
New Castle, DE 19720
Crisis Phone 1: (302) 421-6711
Business Phone: (302) 421-6711

WILMINGTON

Contact Wilmington, Inc.
Washington St. at Lea Blvd.
Wilmington, DE 19802
Crisis Phone 1: (302) 575-1112
Deaf Contact: (302) 656-6660
Business Phone: (302) 762-4989

DISTRICT OF COLUMBIA

WASHINGTON

* Fact Hotline
   (Families and Children in
   Trouble)
Family Stress Services of DC/
   NCPCA
2001 "O" St., NW,
   Suite G-1200
Washington, DC 20036
Crisis Phone 1: (202) 628-3228
Business Phone: (202) 965-1900

WASHINGTON

* St. Francis Center
2633-15th St., NW, Suite #11
Washington, DC 20009
Crisis Phone 1: (202) 234-5613
Business Phone: (202) 234-5613

WASHINGTON

D.C. Suicide Prevention
Crisis Resolution Branch
DC Dept. of Human Services
1905 E St. S.E.
Washington, DC 20005
Crisis Phone 1: (202) 727-3622
Business Phone: (202) 727-3622

FLORIDA

BARTOW

* Crisis Intervention Services
Peace River Center
1745 Highway 17 South
Bartow, FL 33830
Crisis Phone 1: (813) 533-4323
Crisis Phone 2: (800) 282-6342
Business Phone: (813) 533-3141

BRADENTON

Manatee Mental Health Center
Crisis Services
P.O. Box 9478
Bradenton, FL 33506
Crisis Phone 1: (813) 748-8648
Business Phone: (813) 747-8648

FORT LAUDERDALE

Crisis Intervention Center of
   Broward Co.
P.O. Box 7537
Fort Lauderdale, FL 33338
Crisis Phone 1: (305) 323-8553
Business Phone: (305) 763-1213

Ft. Myers

Ft. Myers Crisis Intervention
Center
Lee Mental Health Center
P.O. Box 06137
Ft. Myers, FL 33906
Crisis Phone 1: (813) 332-1477
Business Phone: (813) 334-3537

Ft. Walton Beach

Crisis Line
205 Shell Ave.
Ft. Walton Beach, FL 32548
Crisis Phone 1: (904) 244-9191
Crestview, Toll Free:
  (800) 682-0101
Business Phone: (904) 244-0151
  ext.: 35

Gainesville

*#Alachua County Crisis Center
730 N. Waldo Rd.; Suite #100
Gainesville, FL 32601
Crisis Phone 1: (904) 376-4444
Crisis Phone 2: (904) 376-4445
Business Phone: (904) 372-3659

Jacksonville

* Suicide Prevention Service
2218 Park St.
Jacksonville, FL 32204
Crisis Phone 1: (904) 384-2234
Business Phone: (904) 387-5641

Key West/Monroe County

* Helpline, Inc.
Florida Keys Memorial Hosp.
5900 Junior College Rd.
Key West, FL 33040
Crisis Phone 1: (305) 296-HELP
Crisis Phone 2: (305) 294-LINE

Middle and Upper Keys:
  (800) 341-4343
Business Phone: (305) 294-5531
  ext.: 3412

Miami

* Switchboard of Miami, Inc.
35 S.W. 8th St.
Miami, FL 33130
Crisis Phone 1: (305) 358-4357
Business Phone: (305) 358-1640

Orlando

* Mental Health Services of
Orange
2520 North Orange Ave.
Orlando, FL 32804
Crisis Phone 1: (305) 896-9306
Business Phone: (305) 896-9306

Panama City

Panama City Crisis Line
Northwest Mental Health
Center
615 N. McArthur Ave.
Panama City, FL 32401
Crisis Phone 1: (904) 769-9481
Business Phone: (904) 769-9481

Pensacola

Pensacola Help Line
Lakeview Center, Inc.
1221 W. Lakeview St.
Pensacola, FL 32501
Crisis Phone 1: (904) 438-1617
Business Phone: (904) 432-1222
  ext.: 300

111

HAWAII

HONOLULU/ OAHU

* Suicide and Crisis Center
200 N. Vineyard Blvd.,
Rm. #603
Honolulu, HI 96817
Crisis Phone 1: (808) 521-4555
Business Phone: (808) 536-7234

KAILUA-KONA

Kona Crisis Center, Inc.
P.O. Box 4363
Kailua-Kona, HI 96740
Crisis Phone 1: (808) 329-9111
Business Phone: (808) 329-6744

LIHUE

Helpline Kauai
P.O. Box 3541
Lihue, HI 96766
Crisis Phone 1: (808) 822-4114
Business Phone: (808) 822-7435

WAILUKU

* Helpline/Suicide
and
Crisis Center
Maui Kokua Services, Inc.
95 Mahalani Street
Wailuku, HI 96793
Crisis Phone 1: (808) 244-7407
Business Phone: (808) 244-7405

IDAHO

BOISE

Emergency Line
Region IV Services/Mental
Health
1105 S. Orchard
Boise, ID 83705
Crisis Phone 1: (208) 338-7044
Business Phone: (208) 338-7020

COEUR D' ALENE

Coeur D' Alene Emergency
Line
W. George Moody Health Center
2195 Ironwood Court
Coeur D' Alene, ID 83814
Crisis Phone 1: (208) 667-6406
Business Phone: (208) 667-6406

IDAHO FALLS

Idaho Falls Emergency
Services
Region VII Mental Health
150 Shoup
Idaho Falls, ID 83402
Crisis Phone 1: (208) 525-7129
Business Phone: (208) 525-7129

KELLOGG

Kellogg Emergency Line
Health and Welfare Service
Center
313 W. Cameron
Kellogg, ID 83837
Crisis Phone 1: (208) 667-6406
Crisis Phone 2: (208) 773-2906
Business Phone: (208) 784-1351

TWIN FALLS

Twin Falls Emergency
 Services
Region 5 Mental Health
823 Harrison
Twin Falls, ID 83301
Crisis Phone 1: (208) 734-4000
Business Phone: (208) 734-9770

ILLINOIS

BELLEVILLE

*#Call for Help
 Suicide & Crisis Intervention
 Service
500 Wilshire Dr.
Belleville, IL 62223
Crisis Phone 1: (618) 397-0963
Business Phone: (618) 397-0968

BLOOMINGTON

* Emergency Crisis Intervention
 Team
McLean Co. Center for Human
 Services
108 W. Market
Bloomington, IL 61701
Crisis Phone 1: (309) 827-4005
Business Phone: (309) 827-5351

CAIRO

Cairo Crisis Line
Mental Health Center
218 10th Street
Cairo, IL 62914
Crisis Phone 1: (618) 734-2665
Business Phone: (618) 734-2665

CHAMPAIGN

Champaign Emergency Service
Champaign Mental Health
 Clinic
600 E. Park
Champaign, IL 61820
Crisis Phone 1: (217) 359-4141
Business Phone: (217) 398-8080

CHICAGO

* Society of Samaritans—
 Chicago
5638 S. Woodlawn Ave.
Chicago, IL 60637
Crisis Phone 1: (312) 947-8300
Business Phone: (312) 947-8844

CHICAGO

In Touch Helpline
Student Counseling Service
University of Illinois
P.O. Box 4348
Chicago, IL 60680
Crisis Phone 1: (312) 996-5535
Business Phone: (312) 996-5535

DANVILLE

Contact Danville
504 N. Vermilion
Danville, IL 61832
Crisis Phone 1: (217) 443-2273
Business Phone: (217) 446-8212

EDWARDSVILLE

Edwardsville Community
 Counseling Services
1507 Troy Rd., Suite #3
Edwardsville, IL 62025
Crisis Phone 1: (618) 877-4420
Business Phone: (618) 656-8721

ELGIN

* Community Crisis Center
P.O. Box 1390
Elgin, IL 60121
Crisis Phone 1: (312) 697-2380
Business Phone: (312) 742-4031

ELK GROVE

Talk Line/Kids Line, Inc.
P.O. Box 1321
Elk Grove, IL 60007
Talk Line: (312) 228-6400
Kids Line: (312) 228-KIDS

EVANSTON

Evanston Hospital Crisis Intervention
2650 Ridge Ave.
Evanston, IL 60201
Crisis Phone 1: (312) 492-6500
Business Phone: (312) 492-6500

GALESBURG

* Spoon River Community MHC
302 E. Main Street; Suite #530
Galesburg, IL 61401
Crisis Phone 1: (800) 322-7143
Business Phone: (309) 343-5155

HILLSBORO

Hillsboro Helpline
Montgomery Co. Counseling
Center
200 S. Main St.
Hillsboro, IL 62049
Crisis Phone 1: (217) 532-9581
Crisis Phone 2: (217) 532-6191
Business Phone: (217) 532-9581

JOLIET

Crisis Line of Will County
P.O. Box 2354
Joliet, IL 60435
Crisis Phone 1: (815) 722-3344
Frankfort: (815) 469-6166
Wilmington: (815) 476-6969
Administration: (815) 744-5280
Business Phone: (815) 744-5280

LINCOLN

Lincoln Crisis Clinic
A. Lincoln Mental Health
Center
315 8th
Lincoln, IL 62656
Crisis Phone 1: (217) 732-3500
Business Phone: (217) 732-2161

MT. VERNON

Mt. Vernon Crisis Line
Comprehensive Services
601 N. 18th
P. O. Box 428
Mt. Vernon, IL 62864
Crisis Phone 1: (618) 242-1512
Business Phone: (618) 242-1510

PEORIA

Peoria Call for Help
5407 N. University
Peoria, IL 61614
Crisis Phone 1: (309) 673-7373
Business Phone: (309) 692-1766

ROCKFORD

* Contact Rockford
P.O. Box 1976
Rockford, IL 61110
Crisis Phone 1: (815) 964-4044
Business Phone: (815) 964-0400

WOOD RIVER

* Crisis Services of Madison
  County
  P.O. Box 570
  Wood River, IL 62095
  Crisis Phone 1: (618) 877-4420
  Crisis Phone 2: (618) 463-1058
  Business Phone: (618) 251-4073

INDIANA
EVANSVILLE

* Southwestern Indiana MHC,
  Inc.
  415 Mulberry
  Evansville, IN 47713
  Crisis Phone 1: (812) 423-7791
  Business Phone: (812) 423-7791

FT. WAYNE

Switchboard, Inc.
316 W. Creighton
Ft. Wayne, IN 46807
Crisis Phone 1: (219) 456-4561
Business Phone: (219) 745-7914

GARY

Rap Line—Crisis Center
215 N. Grand Blvd.
Gary, IN 46403
Crisis Phone 1: (219) 980-9243
Business Phone: (219) 980-4207

INDIANAPOLIS

* Mental Health Assoc. in Mar-
  ion Co.
  Crisis & Suicide Intervention
  Service
  1433 N. Meridian St., Rm. #202
  Indianapolis, IN 46202
  Crisis Phone 1: (317) 632-7575
  Business Phone: (317) 269-1569

IOWA
AMES

Open Line
Welch Ave. Station, Box 1138
Ames, IA 50010
Crisis Phone 1: (515) 292-7000
Business Phone: (515) 292-4983

CEDAR RAPIDS

* Foundation 2, Inc.
  1251 Third Ave. SE
  Cedar Rapids, IA 52403
  Crisis Phone 1: (319) 362-2174
  Business Phone: (319) 362-2176

DES MOINES

* Community Telephone Coun-
  seling/Crisis Line
  Service of the American Red
  Cross
  P.O. Box 7067
  Des Moines, IA 50309
  Crisis: (515) 244-1000
  Counseling: (515) 244-1010
  Business Phone: (515) 244-6700

DUBUQUE

Phone A Friend Crisis Line
Suite 420, Nesler Center
Dubuque, IA 52001
Crisis Phone 1: (319) 588-4016
Business Phone: (319) 557-8331

IOWA CITY

Iowa City Crisis Intervention
Center
26 East Market
Iowa City, IA 52240
Crisis Phone 1: (319) 351-0140
Business Phone: (319) 351-2726

Aid Center
406 5th St.
Sioux City, IA 51101
Crisis Phone 1: (712) 252-1861
Business Phone: (712) 252-1861

LOUISIANA

*#Baton Rouge Crisis Interven-
    tion Center
P.O. Box 80738
Baton Rouge, LA 70898
Crisis Phone 1: (504) 924-3900
Business Phone: (504) 924-1595

*   Tangipahoa Crisis Phone, Inc.
P.O. Box 153
Hammond, LA 70404
Crisis Phone 1: (504) 345-6120
Business Phone: (504) 345-5335

*#Mental Health Assoc. of New
    Orleans
Crisis Line Program
2515 Canal St. Ste-200
New Orleans, LA 70119
Crisis Phone 1: (504) 523-2673
Business Phone: (504) 821-1024

*   River Oaks Crisis Center
1525 River Oaks Road W.
New Orleans, LA 70123
Crisis Phone 1: (504) 733-2273
Business Phone: (504) 734-1740

Open Ear
Centenary College
P.O. Box 247
Shreveport, LA 71106
Crisis Phone 1: (318) 869-1228
Business Phone: (318) 869-1228

MAINE

Dial Help
43 Illinois Ave.
Bangor, ME 04401
Crisis Phone 1: (207) 947-6143
Toll Free: (800) 431-7810
Business Phone: (207) 947-6143

*   Ingraham Volunteers, Inc.
142 High St.
Portland, ME 04101
Crisis Phone 1: (207) 774-HELP
TTY/TDD: (207) 773-7321
Business Phone: (207) 773-4830

*   Crisis Stabilization Unit
147 Water St.
Skowhegan, ME 04976

Augusta: (207) 623-4511

Waterville: (207) 872-2276

Skowhegan: (800) 452-1933

Business Phone: (207) 474-2506

MARYLAND

Baltimore

Baltimore Crisis Center
Walter P. Carter MHC
630 W. Fayette St.
Baltimore, MD 21201
Crisis Phone 1: (301) 528-2200
Business Phone: (301) 528-2200

Baltimore

Baltimore Crisis Line
Sinai Hospital
Belvedere and Greenspring Ave.
Baltimore, MD 21215
Weekdays: (301) 578-5457

Evenings & Weekends:
(301) 578-5000

Business Phone: (301) 578-5457

Kensington

*#Montgomery County Hotline
10920 Connecticut Ave.
Kensington, MD 20795
Crisis Phone 1: (301) 949-6603
Business Phone: (301) 949-1255

MASSACHUSETTS

Boston

*#The Samaritans
500 Commonwealth Ave.
Boston, MA 02215
Crisis Phone 1: (617) 247-0220
Business Phone: (617) 536-2460

Fall River

* Samaritans of Fall River-New
  Bedford, Inc.
  386 Stanley St.
  Fall River, MA 02720
  Crisis Phone 1: (617) 636-6111
  Business Phone: (617) 636-6111

Framingham

* Samaritans of South Middle-
  sex, Inc.
  73 Union Ave.
  Framingham, MA 01701
  Crisis Phone 1: (617) 875-4500
  Business Phone: (617) 875-4500

Lawrence

* Psychiatric Associates of
  Lawrence
  42 Franklin St.
  Lawrence, MA 01840
  Crisis Phone 1: (617) 682-7442
  Business Phone: (617) 682-7442

Norwood

*#So. Norfolk Screening and
  Emergency Team
  91 Central St.
  Norwood, MA 02062
  Crisis Phone 1: (617) 769-6060
  Business Phone: (617) 769-6060

Salem

Samaritans of Salem
P.O. Box 8133
Salem, MA 01970
Crisis Phone 1: (617) 744-5000
Business Phone: (617) 744-5000

WORCESTER

* Crisis Center, Inc.
P.O. Box 652
Worcester, MA 01602
Crisis Phone 1: (617) 791-6562
Business Phone: (617) 791-7205

MICHIGAN

ANN ARBOR

Washtenaw County Community MHC
2929 Plymouth Rd.
Ann Arbor, MI 48105
Crisis Phone 1: (313) 996-4747
Business Phone: (313) 994-2285

DETROIT

*#Suicide Prevention Center/
Detroit
220 Bagley, Suite 626
Detroit, MI 48226
Crisis Phone 1: (313) 224-7000
Business Phone: (313) 963-7890

DETROIT

Contact Life Line
7430 2nd St., Rm. #428
Detroit, MI 48202
Crisis Phone 1: (313) 894-5555
Business Phone: (313) 875-0426

EAST LANSING

Listening Ear of East Lansing
547½ E. Grand River
East Lansing, MI 48823
Crisis Phone 1: (517) 337-1717
Business Phone: (517) 337-1717

FLINT

Flint Emergency Service
Genesee County Mental Health
420 W. 5th Ave.
Flint, MI 48503
Crisis Phone 1: (313) 257-3740
Business Phone: (313) 257-3742

HART

* Oceana County Community
Mental Health
P.O. Box 127
Hart, MI 49420
Crisis Phone 1: (616) 873-2108
Business Phone: (616) 873-2108

KALAMAZOO

* Gryphon Place
1104 S. Westnedge
Kalamazoo, MI 49008
Crisis Phone 1: (616) 381-4357
Business Phone: (616) 381-1510

MINNESOTA

GRAND RAPIDS

Nightingale Help Phone
Information and Referral
Service
P.O. Box 113
Grand Rapids, MN 55744
Crisis Phone 1: (218) 326-8565
Business Phone: (218) 326-8565

MINNEAPOLIS

*#Crisis Intervention Center
Hennepin County Medical
Center
701 Park Ave. South
Minneapolis, MN 55415

Crisis: (612) 347-3161
Suicide: (612) 347-2222
Crisis Home Program:
(612) 347-3170
Sexual Assault Service:
(612) 347-5838
Business Phone: (612) 347-3164

MINNEAPOLIS

Contact Twin Cities
83 S. 12th St.
Minneapolis, MN 55403
Crisis Phone 1: (612) 341-2896
Business Phone: (612) 341-2212

WORTHINGTON/LUVERNE/PIPE-
STONE/WINDOM

* 24-Hour Crisis Hotline
Southwestern Mental Health
  Center
1224 Fourth Ave.
Worthington, MN 56187
Crisis Phone 1: (800) 642-1525
Business Phone: (507) 372-7671

MISSISSIPPI

HATTIESBURG

Hattiesburg Help Line, Inc.
P.O. Box 183
Hattiesburg, MS 39401
Crisis Phone 1: (601) 545-HELP
Business Phone: (601) 545-HELP

JACKSON

Contact Jackson
P.O. Box 5192
Jackson, MS 39216
Crisis Phone 1: (601) 969-2077
Business Phone: (601) 969-2077

MERIDIAN

Weems Mental Health Center
P.O. Box 4376 WS
Meridian, MS 39301
Crisis Phone 1: (601) 483-4821
Business Phone: (601) 483-4821

UNIVERSITY

Rapline
P.O. Box 5923
University, MS 38677
Crisis Phone 1: (601) 232-6439
Business Phone: (601) 232-6439

MISSOURI

JOPLIN

Joplin Crisis Intervention, Inc.
P.O. Box 582
Joplin, MO 64801
Crisis Phone 1: (417) 781-2255
Business Phone: (417) 781-2255

KANSAS CITY

K.C. Suicide Prevention Line
Western Missouri Mental
  Health Center
600 E. 22nd St.
Kansas City, MO 64108
Crisis Phone 1: (816) 471-3939
Crisis Phone 2: (816) 471-3940
Business Phone: (816) 471-3000

ST. LOUIS

*#Life Crisis Services, Inc.
1423 S. Big Bend Blvd.
St. Louis, MO 63117
Crisis Phone 1: (314) 647-4357
Business Phone: (314) 647-3100

St. Joseph

St. Joseph Crisis Service
St. Joseph State Hospital
St. Joseph, MO 64506
Crisis Phone 1: (816) 232-8431
Business Phone: (816) 232-8431

MONTANA

Billings

Billings Helpline
Yellowstone Co. Welfare
3021 3rd Avenue N
Billings, MT 59191
Crisis Phone 1: (406) 248-1691
Business Phone: (406) 248-1691

Great Falls

Great Falls Crisis Center
P.O. Box 124
Great Falls, MT 59403
Crisis Phone 1: (406) 453-6512
Business Phone: (406) 453-6512

Helena

Southwest Montana MHC
572 Logan
Helena, MT 59601
Crisis Phone 1: (406) 443-9667
Business Phone: (406) 443-9667

Missoula

Missoula Crisis Center, Inc.
P.O. Box 9345
Missoula, MT 59807
Crisis Phone 1: (406) 543-4555
Business Phone: (406) 543-4555

NEBRASKA

Lincoln

Personal Crisis Service
P.O. Box 80083
Lincoln, NE 68506
Crisis Phone 1: (402) 475-5171
Business Phone: (402) 475-5171

North Platte

North Platte Emergency
  Services
Great Plains Mental Health
  Center
P.O. Box 1209
North Platte, NE 69103
Crisis Phone 1: (308) 532-9332
Business Phone: (308) 532-4050

Omaha

Omaha Personal Crisis
  Service, Inc.
4102 Woolworth Avenue
Omaha, NE 68105
Crisis Phone 1: (402) 444-7335
Business Phone: (402) 444-7335

NEVADA

Las Vegas

Las Vegas Suicide Prevention
  Center
2408 Santa Clara Dr.
Las Vegas, NV 89104
Crisis Phone 1: (702) 732-1622
Business Phone: (702) 732-1600

RENO

* Suicide Prevention & Crisis
  Call Center
  P.O. Box 8016
  Reno, NV 89507
  Crisis Phone 1: (702) 323-6111
  Business Phone: (702) 323-7533

NEW HAMPSHIRE

CLAREMONT

Intake/Crisis/Evaluation Unit
Counseling Center of Sullivan
Co.
18 Bailey Ave.
Claremont, NH 03743
Crisis Phone 1: (603) 542-2578
Business Phone: (603) 542-2578

CONCORD

*#Emergency Services/Concord
CNHCMS, INC.
P.O. Box 2032
Concord, NH 03301
Crisis Phone 1: (603) 228-1551
Business Phone: (603) 228-1551

MANCHESTER

Greater Manchester MHC
  401 Cypress St.
  Manchester, NH 03103
  Crisis Phone 1: (603) 668-4111
  Business Phone: (603) 668-4111

PORTSMOUTH

* Seacoast Mental Health
  Center
  1145 Sagamore Ave.
  Portsmouth, NH 03801
  Crisis Phone 1: (603) 431-6703
  Business Phone: (603) 431-6703

SALEM

Center For Life Management
Salem Prof. Park
14 Stiles Rd.
Salem, NH 03079
Crisis Phone 1: (603) 432-2253
Business Phone: (603) 893-3548

NEW JERSEY

ATLANTIC CITY

Crisis Intervention Program/
AC
Atlantic City Medical Center
1925 Pacific Ave.
Atlantic City, NJ 08401
Crisis Phone 1: (609) 344-1118
Business Phone: (609) 344-1118

CAMDEN

* Emergency and Advocacy
  Services
  Guidance Center of Camden
  Co. Inc.
  1600 Haddon Ave.
  Camden, NJ 08103
  Crisis Phone 1: (609) 428-4357
  Crisis Phone 2: (609) 541-2222
  Business Phone: (609) 428-1300

GLASSBORO

Together, Inc.
7 State St.
Glassboro, NJ 08028
Crisis Phone 1: (609) 881-4040
Business Phone: (609) 881-7045

MONTCLAIR

North Essex Help Line
Mental Health Resource Center
60 S. Fullerton Ave.
Montclair, NJ 07042
Crisis Phone 1: (201) 744-1954
Business Phone: (201) 744-6522

MORRISTOWN

Memo Helpline
100 Madison Ave.
Morristown, NJ 07960
Crisis Phone 1: (201) 540-5045
Business Phone: (201) 540-5168

NEWARK

Newark Emergency Services
Mt. Carmel Guild Community
  MHC
17 Mulberry St.
Newark, NJ 07102
Crisis Phone 1: (201) 596-4100
Business Phone: (201) 596-4100

TOMS RIVER

Contact of Ocean County
P.O. Box 1121
Toms River, NJ 08753
Crisis Phone 1: (201) 240-6100
Business Phone: (201) 240-6104

UNION

Communication—Help Center
Kean College of New Jersey
Morris Avenue
Union, NJ 07083
Crisis Phone 1: (201) 527-2360
Crisis Phone 2: (201) 527-2330
Crisis Phone 3: (201) 289-2101
Business Phone: (201) 289-2100

WEST TRENTON

Contact of Mercer County, NJ,
  Inc.
Katzenbach School for the Deaf
320 Sullivan Way
W. Trenton, NJ 08628
Crisis Phone 1: (609) 883-2880
Business Phone: (609) 883-2880
TTY: (609) 587-3050
TTY: (609) 452-1919

NEW MEXICO

ALBUQUERQUE

Crisis Unit
Bernalillo Co. Mental Health
  Center
2600 Marble N.E.
Albuquerque, NM 87106
Crisis Phone 1: (505) 843-2800
Business Phone: (505) 843-2800

ALBUQUERQUE

AGORA
The Univ. of New Mexico
  Crisis Center
Student Union
P.O. Box 29
Albuquerque, NM 87131
Crisis Phone 1: (505) 277-3013
Business Phone: (505) 277-3013

NEW YORK

ALBANY

Refer Switchboard
Project Equinox
70 Central Avenue
Albany, NY 12210
Crisis Phone 1: (518) 434-1200
Business Phone: (518) 434-1200

ALBANY

Capitol Dist. Psychiatric Center
75 New Scotland Ave.
Albany, NY 12208
Crisis Phone 1: (518) 447-9650
Business Phone: (518) 844-7965

ALBANY

Samaritans of Capitol Dist.
200 Central Ave.
Albany, NY 12206
Crisis Phone 1: (518) 463-2323
Business Phone: (518) 463-0861

BUFFALO

Buffalo Suicide Prevention &
Crisis Services
3258 Main St.
Buffalo, NY 14214
Crisis Phone 1: (716) 834-3131
Business Phone: (716) 834-3131

GOSHEN

Orange County Help Line
Mental Health Association
255 Greenwich Ave.
Goshen, NY 10924
Crisis Phone 1: (914) 343-6906
Crisis Phone 2: (914) 294-9355
Crisis Phone 3: (914) 294-9445
Crisis Phone 4: (914) 342-5871
Crisis Phone 5: (914) 565-6381
Business Phone: (914) 294-7411

ITHACA

*#Suicide Prevention & Crisis
Service
P.O. Box 312
Ithaca, NY 14850
Crisis Phone 1: (607) 272-1616
Business Phone: (607) 272-1505

NEW PALTZ

Oasis
Counseling Center
State Univ. College
New Paltz, NY 12561
Crisis Phone 1: (914) 257-2141
Business Phone: (914) 257-2250

NEW YORK

Help-Line Telephone Services
3 W. 19th Street, Suite #1010
New York, NY 10001
Crisis Phone 1: (212) 532-2400
TTY: (212) 532-0942
Business Phone: (212) 684-4480

NIAGARA FALLS

Niagara Hotline/Crisis Inter-
vention Services
775 3rd St.
Niagara Falls, NY 14302
Crisis Phone 1: (716) 285-3515
Business Phone: (716) 285-9636

QUEENS VILLAGE

Dial-for-Help
Creedmor Psychiatric Center
80-45 Winchester Blvd.
Queens Village, NY 11427
Crisis Phone 1: (212) 464-7515
Business Phone: (212) 464-7500
ext.: 3111

ROCHESTER

* Life Line/Health Assn. of
Rochester
973 East Ave.
Rochester, NY 14607
Crisis Phone 1: (716) 275-5151
Business Phone: (716) 271-3540

STONY BROOK

* Response of Suffolk Co. Inc.
P.O. Box 300
Stony Brook, NY 11790
Crisis Phone 1: (516) 751-7500
Business Phone: (516) 751-7620

SYRACUSE

Suicide Prevention Crisis
  Counseling Services
St. Joseph's Hospital Health
  Center
301 Prospect Ave.
Syracuse, NY 13203
Crisis Phone 1: (315) 474-1333
Business Phone: (315) 474-1333

UTICA

Utica Crisis Intervention
1213 Court St., Cottage 46
Utica, NY 13502
Crisis Phone 1: (315) 736-0883
Rome: (315) 337-7299
Herkimer: (315) 866-0123
Business Phone: (315) 797-6800
  ext.: 4210

WHITE PLAINS

Suicide Prevention Crisis Inter-
  vention Services
MHA of Westchester Co., Inc.
29 Sterling Ave.
White Plains, NY 10606
Suicide Prevention Service:
  (914) 946-0121
Crisis Intervention Service:
  (914) 949-6741
Business Phone: (914) 949-6741

NORTH CAROLINA

ASHVILLE

Contact-Ashville/Buncombe
P.O. Box 6747
Ashville, NC 28816
Crisis Phone 1: (704) 253-4357
Business Phone: (704) 252-7703

BURLINGTON

*#Suicide & Crisis Services/
  Alamance Co.
P.O. Box 2573
Burlington, NC 27215
Crisis Phone 1: (919) 227-6220
Business Phone: (919) 228-1720

CHAPEL HILL

Chapel Hill Helpline
333 MC Masters St.
Chapel Hill, NC 27514
Crisis Phone 1: (919) 929-0479
Business Phone: (919) 929-0479

CHARLOTTE

The Relatives, Inc.
1000 E. Boulevard
Charlotte, NC 28203
Crisis Phone 1: (704) 377-0602
Business Phone: (704) 377-0602

DURHAM

* Helpline of Durham
414 E. Main St.
Durham, NC 27701
Crisis Phone 1: (919) 683-8628
Business Phone: (919) 683-2392

Contact of Fayetteville, Inc.
P.O. Box 456
Fayetteville, NC 28302
Crisis Phone 1: (919) 485-4134
Business Phone: (919) 483-8970

GREENSBORO

Crisis Control Center, Inc.
P.O. Box 735
Greensboro, NC 27402
Crisis Phone 1: (919) 852-4444
Business Phone: (919) 852-6366

RALEIGH

Hopeline, Inc.
P.O. Box 6036
Raleigh, NC 27628
Crisis Phone 1: (919) 755-6555
Business Phone: (919) 755-6555

ROANOKE RAPIDS

Roanoke Rapids Crisis Line
Halifax Co. Mental Health
P.O. Box 1199
Roanoke Rapids, NC 27870
Crisis Phone 1: (919) 537-2909
Business Phone: (919) 537-2909

WINSTON-SALEM

Contact: Winston-Salem
1111 W. First St.
Winston-Salem, NC 27101
Crisis Phone 1: (919) 722-5153
Business Phone: (919) 723-4338

NORTH DAKOTA

BEULAH

* Mercer County Women's
   Resource Center
Hillside Office Complex
Highway 49 NW.
Beulah, ND 58523
Crisis Phone 1: (701) 748-2274
Business Phone: (701) 873-2274

BISMARK

Crisis and Emergency
   Services
West Central Human Service
   Center
600 S. 2nd St.
Bismark, ND 58501
Crisis Phone 1: (701) 255-3090
Business Phone: (701) 255-3090

FARGO

Fargo Hotline
P.O. Box 447
Fargo, ND 58107
Crisis Phone 1: (701) 235-7335
Crisis Phone 2: (701) 232-4357
Business Phone: (701) 293-6462

GRAND FORKS

Grand Forks MH Crisis Line
1407 24th Ave. S.
Grand Forks, ND 58201
Crisis Phone 1: (701) 775-0525
Business Phone: (701) 746-9411

OHIO

AKRON

*#Support, Inc.
1361 W. Market St.
Akron, OH 44313
Crisis Phone 1: (216) 434-9144
Business Phone: (216) 864-7743

ATHENS

Care Line, Inc.
28 W. Stimson
Athens, OH 45701
Crisis Phone 1: (614) 593-3344
Business Phone: (614) 593-3346

CANTON

*#Crisis Intervention Center of
   Stark Co.
2421 13th St., N.W.
Canton, OH 44708
Crisis Phone 1: (216) 452-6000
Business Phone: (216) 452-9812

CINCINNATI

* 281-Care/Talbert House
3891 Reading Rd.
Cincinnati, OH 45206
Crisis Phone 1: (513) 281-2273
Business Phone: (513) 281-2866

COLUMBUS

* Suicide Prevention Services
1301 High
Columbus, OH 43201
Crisis Phone 1: (614) 221-5445
Business Phone: (614) 299-6600

DAYTON

Contact Dayton
P.O. Box 125
Dayton, OH 45459
Crisis Phone 1: (513) 434-6684
Business Phone: (513) 434-1798

DAYTON

*#Suicide Prevention Center, Inc.
184 Salem Ave.
Dayton, OH 45406
Crisis Phone 1: (513) 223-4777
Business Phone: (513) 223-9096

MANSFIELD

Help Line/Adapt
741 Sholl Rd.
Mansfield, OH 44907
Crisis Phone 1: (419) 522-4357
Business Phone: (419) 526-4332

OXFORD

Oxford Crisis & Referral
   Center
111 E. Walnut St.
Oxford, OH 45056
Crisis Phone 1: (513) 523-4146
Business Phone: (513) 523-4148

SPRINGFIELD

Suicide Prevention Center Life-
   Line
1101 East High St.
Springfield, OH 45505
Crisis Phone 1: (513) 322-5433
Business Phone: (513) 328-5300

TOLEDO

* The New Rescue Crisis
  Service
  3314 Collingwood Ave.
  Toledo, OH 43610
  Crisis Phone 1: (419) 255-5500
  Business Phone: (419) 255-5500

TOLEDO

Toledo First Call for Help
1 Stranahan Sq. #141
Toledo, OH 43604
Crisis Phone 1: (419) 244-3728
Business Phone: (419) 244-3728

WOOSTER

Dial A Friend
P.O. Box 303
Wooster, OH 44691
Crisis Phone 1: (216) 262-9999
Business Phone: (216) 262-9499

YOUNGSTOWN

*#Help Hotline, Inc.
P.O. Box 46
Youngstown, OH 44501
Crisis Phone 1: (216) 747-2696
Crisis Phone 2: (216) 424-7767
Crisis Phone 3: (216) 426-9355
TTY: (216) 744-0579
Business Phone: (216) 747-5111

ZANESVILLE

* Six County, Inc. Crisis
  Hotline
  2845 Bell Street
  Zanesville, OH 43701
  Crisis Phone 1: (614) 452-8403
  Business Phone: (614) 454-9766

OKLAHOMA

OKLAHOMA CITY

* Contact of Metro. Oklahoma
  City
  P.O. Box 12832
  Oklahoma City, OK 73157
  Crisis Phone 1: (405) 848-2273
  Business Phone: (405) 840-9396

TULSA

Tulsa Helpline
P.O. Box 52847
Tulsa, OK 74152
Crisis Phone 1: (918) 583-4357
Business Phone: (918) 585-1144

OREGON

EUGENE

Mental Health Emergency
Center/CIRT
151 W. 5th St.
Eugene, OR 97401
Crisis Phone 1: (503) 687-4000
Business Phone: (503) 687-3608

GRANTS PASS

Josephine County Info. & Re-
ferral Services
P.O. Box 670
Grants Pass, OR 97526
Crisis Phone 1: (503) 479-HELP
Business Phone: (503) 479-2349

KLAMATH FALLS

Hope in Crisis
P.O. Box 951
Klamath Falls, OR 97601
Crisis Phone 1: (503) 884-0636
Business Phone: (503) 882-8974

PORTLAND

* Metro Crisis Intervention
  Service
  P.O. Box 637
  Portland, OR 97207
  Crisis Phone 1: (503) 223-6161
  Business Phone: (503) 226-3099

PENNSYLVANIA

ALLENTOWN

Crisis Intervention Team
Lehigh County
512 Hamilton St., Suite #300
Allentown, PA 18101
Crisis Phone 1: (215) 820-3127
Business Phone: (215) 820-3127

ALTOONA

Contact Altoona
P.O. Box 11
Altoona, PA 16603
Crisis Phone 1: (814) 946-9050
Business Phone: (814) 946-0531

BETHLEHEM

Crisis Intervention Team
  (MH/MR)
Northampton County
Broad & New Streets
Bethlehem, PA 18018
Crisis Phone 1: (215) 865-0944
Business Phone: (215) 865-0944

ERIE

Info. & Referral Division
United Way of Erie County
110 W. 10th St.
Erie, PA 16501-1466
Erie Hotline: (814) 453-5656
Business Phone: (814) 456-2937

GETTYSBURG

Adams/Hanover Counseling
  Service
37 West St.
Gettysburg, PA 17325
Crisis Phone 1: (717) 334-9111
Business Phone: (717) 334-9111

HARRISBURG

Contact Harrisburg
P.O. Box 6270
Harrisburg, PA 17112
Crisis Phone 1: (717) 652-4400
Business Phone: (717) 652-4987

LANCASTER

Contact Lancaster
447 E. King St.
Lancaster, PA 17602
Crisis Phone 1: (717) 299-4855
Business Phone: (717) 291-2261

NANTICOKE

Hazelton-Nanticoke Crisis
  Services
Hazelton-Nanticoke MHC
W. Washington St.
Nanticoke, PA 18634
Crisis Phone 1: (717) 735-7590
Business Phone: (717) 735-7590

PHILADELPHIA

Contact Philadelphia
P.O. Box 12586
Philadelphia, PA 19151
Crisis Phone 1: (215) 879-4402
Business Phone: (215) 877-9099

PHILADELPHIA

Philadelphia Suicide & Crisis
  Intervention Center
1 Reading Center
1101 Market, 7th Floor
Philadelphia, PA 19107
Crisis Phone 1: (215) 686-4420
Business Phone: (215) 592-5565

PITTSBURGH

* Helpline/Pittsburgh
200 Ross St.
Pittsburgh, PA 15219
Crisis Phone 1: (412) 255-1155
Business Phone: (412) 255-1133

SCRANTON

Free Info. & Referral System
  Telephone
200 Adams Ave.
Scranton, PA 18503
Crisis Phone 1: (717) 961-1234
Business Phone: (717) 961-1234

WILKES BARRE

Luzerne/Wyoming County
  MH/MR Center #1
103 S. Main St.
Wilkes Barre, PA 18702
Crisis Phone 1: (717) 823-2155
Business Phone: (717) 823-2155

WILLIAMSPORT

Williamsport Helpline
815 W. 4th St.
Williamsport, PA 17701
Crisis Phone 1: (717) 323-8555
Crisis Phone 2: (800) 624-4636
Business Phone: (717) 323-8555

YORK

Contact York
145 S. Duke St.
York, PA 17403
Crisis Phone 1: (717) 845-3656
Business Phone: (717) 845-9125

RHODE ISLAND

PROVIDENCE

* The Samaritans of Providence
33 Chestnut St.
Providence, RI 02903
Crisis Phone 1: (401) 272-4044
Business Phone: (401) 272-4044

WAKEFIELD

Sympatico
29 Columbia St.
Wakefield, RI 02879
Crisis Phone 1: (401) 783-0650
Business Phone: (401) 783-0782

SOUTH CAROLINA

COLUMBIA

* Helpline of Midland, Inc.
P.O. Box 6336
Columbia, SC 29260
Crisis Phone 1: (803) 771-4357
Business Phone: (803) 799-6329

GREENVILLE

Help-Line/Greenville
P.O. Box 1085
Greenville, SC 29602
Crisis Phone 1: (803) 233-HELP
Business Phone: (803) 242-0955

SOUTH DAKOTA

ABERDEEN

New Beginnings Center
1206 North Third
Aberdeen, SD 57401
Crisis Phone 1: (605) 229-1239
Business Phone: (605) 229-1239

SIOUX FALLS

Community Crisis Line
313 S. 1st Ave.
Sioux Falls, SD 57102
Crisis Phone 1: (605) 334-7022
Business Phone: (605) 334-7022

TENNESSEE

CHATTANOOGA

Contact of Chattanooga
1202 Duncan
Chattanooga, TN 37404
Crisis Phone 1: (615) 266-8228
Crisis Phone 2: (615) 622-5193
Business Phone: (615) 629-0039

JOHNSON CITY

Contact Ministries
P.O. Box 1403
Johnson City, TN 37601
Crisis Phone 1: (615) 926-0144
Business Phone: (615) 926-0140

KNOXVILLE

Contact Telephone of Knoxville
P.O. Box 11234
Knoxville, TN 37939-1234
Crisis Phone 1: (615) 523-9124
Business Phone: (615) 523-9108

MEMPHIS

* Suicide/Crisis Intervention Services/Memphis
P.O. Box 40068
Memphis, TN 38104
Crisis Phone 1: (901) 274-7477
Business Phone: (901) 276-1111

NASHVILLE

*#Crisis Intervention Center, Inc.
P.O. Box 120934
Nashville, TN 37212
Crisis Phone 1: (615) 244-7444
Business Phone: (615) 298-3359

OAK RIDGE

Contact of Oak Ridge
P.O. Box 641
Oak Ridge, TN 37830
Crisis Phone 1: (615) 482-4949
Business Phone: (615) 482-4940

TEXAS

AMARILLO

* Suicide Prevention/Crisis Intervention Center
P.O. Box 3250
Amarillo, TX 79106
Crisis Phone 1: (806) 376-4251
Toll Free In-State: (800) 692-4039
Business Phone: (806) 353-7235

AUSTIN

Information Hotline & Crisis Center
102 Neches
Austin, TX 78705
Crisis Phone 1: (512) 472-HELP
Business Phone: (512) 475-5695

* Rape & Suicide Crisis of SE
  Texas
  P.O. Box 5011
  Beaumont, TX 77706
  Crisis Phone 1: (409) 835-3355
  Business Phone: (409) 832-6530

* Crisis Services/Corpus Christi
  4906-B Everhart
  Corpus Christi, TX 78411
  Crisis Phone 1: (512) 993-7410
  Business Phone: (512) 993-7416

*#Suicide & Crisis Center
  2808 Swiss Ave.
  Dallas, TX 75204
  Crisis Phone 1: (214) 828-1000
  Business Phone: (214) 824-7020

*#Tarrant County Crisis Inter-
  vention
  % Family Service, Inc.
  716 Magnolia
  Ft. Worth, TX 76104
  Crisis Phone 1: (817) 336-3355
  Business Phone: (817) 336-0108

*#Crisis Intervention of Houston,
  Inc.
  P.O. Box 13066
  Houston, TX 77219
  Central: (713) 228-1505
  Bay Area: (713) 333-5111
  Business Phone: (713) 527-9426

Contact Lubbock
P.O. Box 6477
Lubbock, TX 79493-6477
Crisis Phone 1: (806) 765-8393
Teen Line: (806) 765-7272
Business Phone: (806) 765-7272

Plano Crisis Center
P.O. Box 1808
Plano, TX 75074
Crisis Phone 1: (214) 881-0088
Business Phone: (214) 881-0081

* United Way Help Line
  P.O. Box 898
  San Antonio, TX 78293-0898
  Crisis Phone 1: (512) 227-4357
  Business Phone: (512) 224-5000

UTAH

Logan Helpline
121 A UMC Utah State Univ.
Logan, UT 84322
Crisis Phone 1: (801) 752-3964
Business Phone: (801) 752-1702

Ogden Emergency Services
Weber County MHC
2510 Washington Blvd., 5th Fl.
Ogden, UT 84401
Crisis Phone 1: (801) 626-9270
Business Phone: (801) 626-9100

PROVO

* Utah County Crisis Line
P.O. Box 1375
Provo, UT 84603
Crisis Phone 1: (801) 226-8989
Business Phone: (801) 226-8989

SALT LAKE CITY

Salt Lake City Crisis Interven-
tion
#50 N. Medical Dr.
Salt Lake City, UT 84132
Crisis Phone 1: (801) 581-2296
Business Phone: (801) 581-2296

VERMONT

BRATTLEBORO

Hotline for Help, Inc.
17 Elliot St.
Brattleboro, VT 05301
Crisis Phone 1: (802) 257-7989
Business Phone: (802) 257-7980

RANDOLPH

Orange County MH Service
  Emergency Service
P.O. Box G
Randolph, VT 05060
Crisis Phone 1: (802) 728-9641
Business Phone: (802) 728-3230

ST. ALBANS

St. Albans Emergency & Crisis
  Service
Franklin Grand Isle MH Ser-
  vice, Inc.
8 Ferris Street
St. Albans, VT 05478
Crisis Phone 1: (802) 524-6554
Business Phone: (802) 524-6554

VIRGINIA

ALEXANDRIA

Alexandria C.A.I.R. Hotline
418 S. Washington St.,
  Suite 101
Alexandria, VA 22314
Crisis Phone 1: (703) 548-3810
Business Phone: (703) 548-0010

ARLINGTON

*#Northern Virginia Hotline
P.O. Box 187
Arlington, VA 22210
Crisis Phone 1: (703) 527-4077
Business Phone: (703) 522-4460

NEWPORT NEWS

Contact Peninsula
211 32nd St.
Newport News, VA 23607
Crisis Phone 1: (804) 245-0041
Business Phone: (804) 861-0330

PORTSMOUTH

* Suicide-Crisis Center, Inc.
P.O. Box 1493
Portsmouth, VA 23705
Crisis Phone 1: (804) 399-6393
Business Phone: (804) 393-0502

ROANOKE

Trust: Roanoke Valley Trouble
  Center
360 Washington Ave.
Roanoke, VA 24016
Crisis Phone 1: (703) 563-0311
Business Phone: (703) 345-8859

WASHINGTON

Crisis Clinic/Thurston &
  Macon County
P.O. Box 2463
Olympia, WA 98507
Crisis Phone 1: (206) 352-2211
Business Phone: (206) 754-3888

RICHLAND

* Mid Columbia Psych. Hospital
    & MHC
  Dial Help
  1175 Gribble
  Richland, WA 99352
  Crisis Phone 1: (509) 943-9104
  Business Phone: (509) 943-9104

SEATTLE

*#Crisis Clinic
  1530 Eastlake East
  Seattle, WA 98102
  Crisis Phone 1: (206) 447-3222
  Business Phone: (206) 447-3210

SPOKANE

Spokane Crisis Services
Spokane City Community MH
S. 107 Division
Spokane, WA 99202
Crisis Phone 1: (509) 838-4428
Business Phone: (509) 838-4651

TACOMA

Tacoma Crisis Clinic
P.O. Box 5007
Tacoma, WA 98405
Crisis Phone 1: (206) 759-6700
Business Phone: (206) 756-5250

YAKIMA

Open Line/Yakima
Central Washington Compre-
  hensive MH
P.O. Box 959
Yakima, WA 98907
Crisis Phone 1: (509) 575-4200
Statewide Toll Free: (800) 572-
  8122
Business Phone: (509) 575-4084

WEST VIRGINIA

CHARLESTON

Contact Kanawha Valley
Christ Church United
  Methodist
Quarrier & Morris Sts.
Charleston, WV 25301
Crisis Phone 1: (304) 346-0826
Business Phone: (304) 346-0828

HUNTINGTON

Contact Huntington
520 11th St.
Huntington, WV 25701
Crisis Phone 1: (304) 523-3448
Business Phone: (304) 523-3447

WHEELING

Upper Ohio Valley Crisis
  Hotline
P.O. Box 653
Wheeling, WV 26003
Crisis Phone 1: (304) 234-8161
Business Phone: (304) 234-1848

WISCONSIN

Eau Claire

* Suicide Prevention Center
1221 Whipple St.
Eau Claire, WI 54701
Crisis Phone 1: (715) 834-6040
Business Phone: (715) 839-3274

Green Bay

C.I.C./Manitowoc Area
131 So. Madison St.
Green Bay, WI 54301
Crisis Phone 1: (414) 682-9172
Business Phone: (414) 432-7855

Madison

* Dane County MHC Emergency
  Services
31 S. Henry
Madison, WI 53703
Crisis Phone 1: (608) 251-2345
Business Phone: (608) 251-2341

Milwaukee

* Milwaukee County CI Service
Mental Health Emergency
  Services
8700 W. Wisconsin Ave. K Rd.
Milwaukee, WI 53226
Crisis Phone 1: (414) 257-7222
Business Phone: (414) 257-7222

Oshkosh

Crisis Intervention Center/
  Oshkosh
P.O. Box 1411
Oshkosh, WI 54902
Crisis Phone 1: (414) 722-7707
Crisis Phone 2: (414) 233-7707
Business Phone: (414) 233-7709

WYOMING

Casper

* Casper Suicide Prevention
Family Support Group
  Assoc., Inc.
611 Thelm Dr.
Casper, WY 82609
Crisis Phone 1: (307) 234-5061
Business Phone: (307) 234-5061

Cheyenne

Cheyenne Helpline
P.O. Box 404
Cheyenne, WY 82001
Crisis Phone 1: (307) 634-4469
Business Phone: (307) 632-4132

CANADA

Alberta

Aid Service of Edmonton
203-10711 107th Avenue
Edmonton, AB T5H OW6
Phone 1: (403) 426-3242/
  426-4252

British Columbia

Crisis Intervention & Suicide
  Prevention
1946 West Broadway
Vancouver, BC
Phone 1: (604) 733-1171/
  228-3700

Manitoba

Klinic Inc.
545 Broadway Avenue
Winnipeg, MB R3C OW3
Phone 1: (204) 786-6943/
  786-8686

NEW BRUNSWICK

Chimo Help Centre Inc.
P.O. Box 1033
Fredericton, NB E3B 5C2
Phone 1: (506) 454-4262/
 455-9464

NORTHWEST TERRITORIES

Help Information & Distress
 Centre
P.O. Box 2580
Yellowknife, NT XOE 1HO
Phone : (403) 873-3190

NOVA SCOTIA

Help Line c/o Dalhousie Uni-
 versity
Cobur Road at Oxford Street
Halifax, NS
Phone 1: (902) 442-2048/422-7444

ONTARIO

Youth Line—Huntley Youth
 Services
34 Huntley Street
Toronto, ON M4L 2Y1
Phone 1: (416) 967-1773/
 922-1700

QUEBEC

Tel-Aide Inc.
C.P. 205, Succursale "H"
Montreal, PQ H3G 2K7
Phone 1: (514) 935-1105/
 935-1101

SASKATCHEWAN

Prince Albert Mobile Crisis
 Unit Co-op
1100-1st Avenue East
Prince Albert, SK S6V 2A7
Phone 1: (306) 764-1011

*Member, American Association of Suicidology
#AAS Certified

This is not a comprehensive list of crisis centers. If you do not find a listing for your area, contact the American Association of Suicidology (2459 South Ash; Denver, Colorado 80222; 303/692-0985) for the name of the closest center. For crisis centers in Canada, contact Distress Centres & Survivor Support Program (Box 393, Postal Station K, Toronto, Ontario M4P 2G7; 416/486-6766).

SUGGESTIONS
FOR
FURTHER READING
AND
VIEWING

BOOKS

Anderson, Luleen, S., *Sunday Came Early This Week*. Cambridge, Massachusetts: Schenkmah, 1982.

Elkind, David, *The Hurried Child: Growing Up Too Fast Too Soon*. Reading, Massachusetts: Addison-Welsey, 1981.

Faucher, Elizabeth, *Surviving: A Novelization*. New York: Scholastic, 1985.

Giffin, Mary, and Felsenthal, Carol, *A Cry for Help*. Garden City, New York: Doubleday, 1983.

Giovacchini, Peter, *The Urge to Die: Why Young People Commit Suicide*. New York: Penguin, 1983.

Hendin, Herbert, *Suicide in America*. New York: Norton, 1984.

Hewitt, John H., *After Suicide*. Philadelphia: Westminster, 1980.

Husain, Syed, and Vandiver, Trish, *Suicide in Children and Adolescents*. New York: Special Medical and Scientific Books, 1984.

Klagsburn, Francine, *Too Young to Die: Youth and Suicide*. New York: Pocket Books, 1984.

Mack, John E. and Hickler, Holly, *Vivienne: The Life and Suicide of an Adolescent Girl*. New York: New American Library, 1982.

Madison, Arnold, *Suicide and Young People*. Boston: Clarion/Houghton Mifflin, 1981.

McCoy, Kathleen, *Coping with Teenage Depression: A Parent's Guide*. New York: New American Library, 1982.

Peck, Michael L., Farberow, Norman L., and Litman, Robert E., *Youth Suicide*. New York: Springer, 1985.

Rabkin, Brenda, *Growing Up Dead: A Hard Look at Why Adolescents Commit Suicide*. Nashville: Abingdon, 1983.

Rosenfeld, Linda, and Prupas, Marilynne, *Left Alive: After a Suicide Death in the Family*. Springfield, Illinois: Charles C. Thomas, 1984.

Shneidman, Edwin S., and Farberow, Norman L., eds., *Clues to Suicide*. New York: McGraw-Hill, 1957.

Sudak, Howard S., Ford, Amasa B., and Rushforth, Norman B., *Suicide in the Young*. Littleton, Massachusetts: PSG Publishing, 1984.

FILMS AND VIDEOTAPES

Adolescent Suicide: A Matter of Life and Death. American Association for Counseling and Development, 5999 Stevenson Avenue, Alexandria, Virginia 22304.

Childhood's End: A Look at Adolescent Suicide. Filmmakers Library, 133 East 50th Street, New York, New York 10022.

Did Jenny Have to Do: Preventing Teen Suicide: You Can Help. Sunburst Communications, 39 Washington Avenue, Room GN-2, Pleasantville, New York 10570.

The Last Cry for Help. (A Learning Corporation Film) Simon and Schuster Communications, 108 Wilmont Road, Deerfield, Illinois 60015.

Sudden Adolescent Death. Human Relations Media, 175 Tompkins Avenue, Pleasantville, New York 10570.

Suicide: Causes and Prevention, same as above.

Teenage Suicide. (MTI Teleprograms, Inc.) Simon and Schuster Communications, 108 Wilmont Road, Deerfield, Illinois 60015.

INDEX